# TWENTY-FIRST CENTURY BLACKJACK: A NEW STRATEGY FOR A NEW MILLENNIUM

By

Walter Thomason

Introduction By Frank Scoblete

*Bonus Books, Inc.*
*Chicago, IL*

This book is not intended to encourage people to gamble. If you or anyone you know has a gambling problem, call 1-800-GAMBLER.

The opinions and conclusions expressed in this book are those of the author, based upon his personal experience and research.

04  03  02  01  00                                              6  5  4  3  2

ISBN 1-56625-132-X
Library of Congress Catalog Card Number: 99-61378


Bonus Books, Inc.
160 East Illinois Street
Chicago, IL 60611                                    .

*First Edition*

*Printed in the United States of America*

# CONTENTS

# ACKNOWLEDGMENTS

My thanks to Fred Renzey — author of *The Blackjack Bluebook,* consultant, columnist, expert blackjack player, and friend.  His knowledge and advice was crucial to the initial framework of this publication.

Thanks to other casino gaming experts — Henry Tamburin, John Grochowski, and "Bootlegger" — who took the time and effort to read the initial manuscript, question the nature of my conjectures, provide additional resources that could support or refute my opinions, and improve the quality of this book.

Most of all, my thanks to Frank Scoblete, the best-selling author of casino gaming books in the United States, who took the time to review the initial manuscript, and contributed greatly to the clarity and accuracy of the final draft.  His book — *Best Blackjack* (Bonus Books, 1996) — is one of the few publications on the market that helps *all of us* to improve our chances of making money while playing this game. His introductory comments regarding this book are most appreciated.

Also, thanks to Steve Bourie, Lee Skelton, and Tex Tracy, who helped with actual casino "field tests" of the betting systems.

And special thanks to Cynthia, my wife, who took time from her writing endeavors to read and correct my lousy grammar, and my son John, who copied documents, corrected spelling errors, and showed me how to work my computer. Every writer should have such a family . . .

# PREFACE

This may be the most unusual book you'll ever read about the game of blackjack.

For the past 30 years practically every reputable book about the game has concluded that counting cards is the only way a player has a long-term chance of winning.

This book presents a radical departure from this conclusion and, based on preliminary studies, 5,000 consecutive hands of actual play, additional studies with over 4,000 hands of actual play, real casino "field tests," computer simulations, and additional verification for other casino gaming experts, proposes *a betting system that can be superior to card counting or flat betting.*

I won't blame you if you are skeptical of the previous statement. But I will blame you if you're not open-minded enough to accept that there might be a viable alternative to counting cards — one that requires much less mental strain, a smaller bankroll, and one that produces a higher frequency of winning sessions.

Don't pre-judge. Read the book. Consider the validity of the 5,000-hand sample that is the basis of most of my calculations and conclusions. Study the results obtained from thousands of hands of additional play. Study the results of the various types of betting systems analyzed, and my explanation as to why my preferred system is superior to others for the large majority of players, *including* card counters.

If you accept what you read and have trust in

the validity of my research, do what I do — try Positive Progressive betting, and enjoy winning for a change!

# INTRODUCTION

For years advocates of "positive" progressive betting have claimed that their system of wagering — that is, increasing your bet as you win — was superior to flat betting at blackjack. For years the only proof they could offer was the logic of their arguments and the persuasiveness of their writing styles. In short, they had no proof. They had no data. They had only their opinions to pit against the mountains of math that showed quite clearly that progressive betting doesn't work any better than flat betting at blackjack.

Played according to the correct Basic Strategy as derived from computer studies, the math shows that blackjack flat bettors and blackjack progressive bettors will lose the same amount of money in the long run despite their different betting styles. The house edge of one-half percent (the approximate edge in multiple-deck games) will take its toll. Of course, the math shows that the pattern of the progressive bettor's losses will be different than the pattern of the flat bettor's losses because his bets are different, but the overall results will be the same.

Traditional gaming writers, myself among them, have dismissed any and all claims that positive progressive betting systems are worthy of serious study because, well, because they *can't* work. You bet money at blackjack, you play Basic Strategy, you lose one-half percent of your total action and that is that! Simple. Clear. Clean. Elegant . . . and, according to Walter Thomason, the author of the book you are reading, *wrong!*

While Thomason's thesis is the same as advocates of progressive betting systems in the past, his *modus operandi* of proving his contentions is radically different and, I believe, attention must be paid to his results. Thomason attempts to prove his case not just by logic but by extensive data recorded over many thousands of decisions dealing actual hands from a shoe, with "field tests" in casinos, and ending with the simulation of hundreds of thousands of hands on a new computer program that can do something no computer program has ever been able to do in blackjack.

Thomason started this study by choosing a unique and incredibly time-consuming three-way comparison of a Basic Strategy player who flat bets, a Basic Strategy player who counts cards and varies his bets according to the count, and a Basic Strategy player who uses Thomason's Four-Step Positive Progressive System. "What's so unique about this study?" you ask. "Haven't studies and computer simulations been done to death on progressive systems in the past?" Not the way Thomason has done it! He has each of these players facing the *exact same dealer* and playing the *exact same hands* against the *exact same dealer hands* with each player utilizing his particular betting system! To my knowledge, this has never been done before.

I can put this in a proper perspective that clearly illuminates the fantastic job Thomason has done by using an analogous situation.

Is Babe Ruth or Mark McGwire the better home run hitter? Oh, you could argue this until you were blue in the face . . .

● *Ruth had to hit a dead ball. McGwire hit a juiced ball.*

● *Ruth hit against inferior pitching because there were no relief specialists. He hit tired pitchers. McGwire hit against fresh pitchers.*

● *Players of yesteryear were better because there were fewer major league teams.*

● *Players today are better because there are many more people in America and athletic training is much, much better.*

● *Ruth was a big fat pig who trained on hot dogs and beer. He couldn't possibly compete with today's athletes.*

● *McGwire took performance-enhancing drugs.*

● *You're ugly!*

● *So are you!*

. . . and you can't approach an answer. You can only argue logic and get nasty when your opponent won't see the rightness of your logic.

But what if Babe Ruth and Mark McGwire could face the *same exact pitchers* and the *same exact pitches*? So the same exact fast ball, in the exact same location, and the exact same curve breaking at the exact same angle that were pitched to Ruth would be pitched to McGwire. In fact, what if every single pitch that Ruth faced in his entire career were also thrown to McGwire and the exact same pitches that McGwire faced were now thrown to Ruth? Wouldn't that solve the dilemma of who was the better home run hitter? Wouldn't it at least go a long way to arriving at a conclusion that most everyone, except perhaps the diehard fans of one or the other, could accept? You bet it would.

That is what Walter Thomason has done. By having his players utilize the same exact Basic

Strategy, playing the exact same hands exactly the same way, against the exact same dealer hands, and making the only difference their respective betting strategies, Walter has figuratively put Ruth and McGwire up against the exact same pitches to see who is better. Needless to say, the results are interesting and, if duplicated by others in the future, downright shocking, and definitely worthy of your attention.

Certainly Thomason has not found the magical, mystical system that will allow you to quit your job and loll around casino venues throughout America and the world. No one will be served peeled grapes by pool side, or eat gourmet every night, or tool around town in a custom-made car due to phenomenal wins accomplished by Thomason's Four-Step Positive Progressive Betting System. What Thomason's data clearly shows is that his system of betting is superior to flat betting for the Basic Strategy player. More importantly, players who utilize the full system Walter advocates, including the "Quit Points" strategy, will dramatically reduce their exposure to the grinding effects of the house edge and, perhaps, dramatically increase their chances to win.

Although you will note that in Thomason's initial 5,000-hand dealt study, the Basic Strategy progressive bettor lost significantly less than either the flat bettor or the card counter, Thomason has not proven that his method of betting is superior to card counting. Nor is he trying to prove that. The card counter, as many readers know, looks for advantageous times to place big bets, advantageous being defined as times when the card counter has an edge. The card counter's loss in the initial study is really the equivalent of a couple or three big bets in a high count. A slight change in "luck" or, as the mathematicians say, a more positive "fluctuation," and the card counter is ahead. In fact the same argument could be made for the progressive bettor as well. A net loss that is equivalent to a single second-step bet in the progression could easily be reversed by Lady Luck. But the poor flat bettor is up against the wall as he's behind over 30 bets! In fact, Thomason's study clearly shows that the flat bettor is behind approximately one-half percent of his total action at the end of 5,000 hands — just what the math predicts! However, unlike the progressive bettor and the card counter, the flat bettor has no way to make a score because he can't increase his bet in favorable situations as the card counter does, and he can't increase his bet hoping for a winning streak as the progressive bettor does.

Of course, 5,000 hands of blackjack are inadequate to make sweeping generalizations about the game of blackjack and Thomason knew this. So he pursued other avenues. He invited skeptics, most of whom are dyed-in-the-wool card counters, such as Fred Renzey, John Grochowski, and Bootlegger to run some shoes to see if different patterns emerged. He could trust these individuals to record the data honestly because they had no vested interest in seeing progressive betting succeed. (And they are all scrupulously honest men as I can attest to.) In each and every hand-dealt series of games, the results were startlingly the same as Thomason's initial 5,000-hand study — the progressive bettor fared better than the flat bettor by a significant margin.

He also conducted several "field tests" in casinos, and invited gaming expert Steve Bourie to witness and record the results of play. Results of

these actual casino gaming experiences further en-
hanced the credibility of his previous findings.

Thomason was ready to publish his findings
after the first 5,000 hands because the data merely
confirmed what his play for several years (and he
plays often) had told him — his system was superior
to flat betting! Several gaming writers told him that
5,000 hands does not a study make. Nor does a few
thousand hands played by other experts, or a few
field trips to the casino. Of course, this elicited a
groan (a sustained grown: aaarrrrggghhhhh!) from
him. Doing 5,000 hand-dealt decisions and recording and analyzing the data had taken the better part
of a year! Blackjack expert Fred Renzey wanted
him to do 100,000 hands. I wanted him to do
20,000 hands. I think gaming experts Henry Tamburin and John Grochowski wanted him to do
something in between. I think Bootlegger wanted
him to forget the whole idea. I think his wife
wanted to kill him! ("Walter, will you get these
charts and graphs off the kitchen table and off the
bed and off the bathroom counter! I haven't seen
the dog in days, and where do I find him? — trying
to gnaw his way out from under a pile of blackjack
spread sheets!)

Then Lady Luck entered the picture in the
form of a computer programmer whose moniker is
"I. B. Winner." Working with Walter, Winner created a program that could do what no other blackjack program had ever done — the exact same
comparisons that Thomason was so laboriously
doing by hand. A player flat betting could be compared to a player betting progressively and a player
betting according to the count against the exact
same hands! Instead of doing another 5,000 or
10,000 decisions, Walter was able to do several

hundreds of thousands of decisions, and you know what? Well, I'm not going to tell you. Read the book. That's why you bought it.

But here are some things I will tell you. If you are a successful card counter, Thomason's system will be of academic interest only (although you may wish to use it for "camouflage" purposes). Why change what works in theory and in practice so well? However, if you are a flat bettor, or an unsuccessful card counter frustrated with your mounting losses at multiple-deck games, give Thomason's system serious consideration. But what if Thomason is wrong? What if in future and bigger studies it turns out that the blackjack math is right in reality as it is right in theory, and that Thomason has been tilting at windmills with initial success but long-term failure? It doesn't matter! Betting Thomason's way will not hurt overall prospects at the game of blackjack. If you are, for example, a $50 flat bettor and you go to his $20, $30, $40, $50 progression — you'll actually save money in the long run since you will be betting less! If the math prevails over the man, you will lose one-half of one percent of all your action — same as the flat bettor. But if the man is right, and for some as yet unexplained reason the Thomason Four-Step Betting System with "Quit Points" actually works in long-term reality, then you will be way ahead of the game.

Fred Renzey, a card counter extraordinaire, looked at Thomason's initial findings and said: "This is disturbing." This *is* disturbing — and exciting! Read on.

— Frank Scoblete

# FOREWORD

The overall objective of this book is simple: Determine which of several different betting systems is most beneficial to the blackjack player.

All of the responsible literature on this game that has been published in the last 30 years states that there are three ways to bet on blackjack:

1. Bet the same amount on every hand, and play perfect Basic Strategy.
2. Bet different amounts on each hand, based on card counting.
3. Bet different amounts on each hand, based on a progressive betting system.

By comparing the win/loss results of play for a "flat" bettor, a "progressive" bettor, and a card counter as applied to 5,000 consecutively dealt hands of play, much can be said about which type of betting system wins more (or loses less) for the player. If every player plays the same hands, in the same order of play, a comparison of the overall outcome should suggest which type of wagering system is most profitable. If additional studies support the conclusions reached in the original study, so much the better!

Those of you who are knowledgeable and educated blackjack players are probably thinking, "Why bother? Everyone knows that card counting is the *only* way to gain a small edge over the casino, that a flat bettor — one who bets the same amount on every hand — will in the long run lose about one-half percent of his wagers, and that the progressive bettor will lose as much as the flat bettor."

Based on the vast majority of the reputable literature currently available, you have good reason to pose the question, "Why bother?"

Why bother, indeed? Why bother to find a viable alternative to card counting if the "experts" tell us there isn't one? As this book progresses I'll explain why I conducted this comparative analysis. I'll explain the different wagering options available, and the procedure used to compare them to each other. And, most importantly, I'll show you the numbers and percentages generated as a result of this study. We will look at money won or lost, rather than statistical formulas, correlation coefficients, deviations from the mean, and nine billion hand-computer-generated projections.

I'll explain why many authors of blackjack books reject the concept of progressive betting, and I'll tell you why I disagree with their opinions.

I'll show you that Positive Progressive betting is more profitable than flat betting, easier and less stressful than card counting, and requires a smaller bankroll than the other two betting systems.

I suspect that if you are a knowledgeable player, you will be skeptical and suspicious of the conclusions reached as a result of my analysis. You'll most likely be left with one of three choices:

1. Assume that I fabricated the 5,000 hands of play, misinterpreted the data from additional studies, altered the results on some hands, misplayed hands, or incorrectly calculated the mathematics. If you believe this, you will no doubt discount the content of this book.

2. Assume that my findings may have some

validity, and seek out other sources that may prove or disprove my conclusions.

3. Assume that my findings are philosophically and mathematically correct, and totally alter your perception of how the game of blackjack should be played.

It's my sincere hope that you select either the second or third choice of action. I strongly believe that you will benefit emotionally and financially by correctly reacting to the information presented.

# Chapter One
# HISTORICAL PERSPECTIVE

Blackjack has been America's most popular casino table game for over thirty years, surpassing the games of craps and roulette after Edward O. Thorp's book, *Beat The Dealer,* became a best seller in the early '60s. He showed us that the average player could learn a basic strategy and card counting system that could give him an *actual advantage* over the casino. He and other statistical experts and casino gaming authors convinced the general public that card counting was the *only* way to go, and research and literature about other methods of play that could be beneficial to the recreational blackjack player generally fell by the wayside.

Today, most casino gaming literature still expounds the virtues of Thorp's original concepts, many of which have been updated and refined to cope with modern casino blackjack.

I began as a recreational player of casino blackjack in 1969. I learned the basic rules, and at that time was an "inspirational" bettor. I played the game and raised or lowered my bets based on "gut feeling." Needless to say, I lost consistently.

Because I enjoyed the challenge of the game, I decided to see what the experts had to say about how to improve my chances of winning. After reading several books on the subject it became obvious that Basic Strategy — a set of rules telling me when to stand, hit, split, or double down — was the cornerstone to building a successful method of play.

Card counting seemed too complicated and my bankroll was limited, so I became a Basic Strategy player who made the same initial wager on each and every hand. In other words, I was a "red chip" player, and never considered risking more than $5 a hand unless splits and double downs required me to increase my bet.

My percentage of winning sessions improved — I didn't lose *all* the time — but I was still losing money *most* of the time, so I attempted to learn card counting.

It wasn't a pleasant experience. After several weeks of practice at home, I attempted to use a simple Hi-Lo system in the casinos. After many sessions of play, all of which resulted in losses, I concluded that counting wouldn't work for me. I was easily distracted and often lost my count. The casinos where I played all used six-deck shoes and only dealt about 65% of the cards before reshuffling. I was afraid to increase my initial wager by more than four times because my bankroll was still limited. I developed headaches after an hour or so of play, mainly due to poor eyesight (bifocals!) and the level of concentration required. I was very uncomfortable with the requirement that I make a 200% increase in my wager because I theoretically had a 1% advantage over the dealer, especially when I had lost the previous hand in spite of a very positive card count! Simply stated, I was losing, losing, losing, and I wasn't having any fun!

As luck would have it, I chanced upon a book, *Progression Blackjack*, by Donald Dahl, in which he proposed a system of increasing the amount of the bet after a winning hand and reverting to a base bet after a losing hand. Even though his plan was not supported by pages of charts, formulas, and verifiable statistics, it seemed reasonable to me. After all — nothing else worked, so why not try something different?

My win/loss results were changed dramatically by using a progressive system. The number of winning sessions increased, as well as the amount won per session. Losing sessions drained my bankroll from time to time, but profits exceeded losses when I stuck to the routine required by a progressive system of betting.

During the last six years I've experimented with many variations to the plan proposed by Mr. Dahl and other progressive betting proponents. I've made several modifications to the systems that they recommend, including the introduction of "Quit Points" — a departure from play which is simple to apply and very profitable! More about this later . . .

In 1993 I began writing about my favorite hobby and self-published a casino travel book and a pamphlet about blackjack. In 1997 my first casino gaming book, *The Ultimate Blackjack Book: Basic Strategies, Money Management, And More*, was published by Carol Publishing Group, an international publisher and the second largest publisher of non-fiction books in the world. This book was quickly followed by *The Experts' Guide to Casino Games*, a basic guidebook for all forms of casino gambling written by many of the most respected experts in the field. *Blackjack For The Clueless*, a compilation of parts from both previous books, was published in 1998.

I've also written dozens of articles for several different magazines, newspapers, and news letters, including *Midwest Gaming and Travel*, *Gulf Coast Casino News*, and Frank Scoblete's *Chance & Cir-*

*cumstance,* and have hosted or been a guest on talk radio programs in Mississippi and Florida.

The preceding information about my background and credentials is *not* presented to convince you to buy my books, or to accept the conclusions reached in this book based on my reputation. My purpose *is* to convince you that I'm a serious student of the game of blackjack, take pride in the integrity of my research, and am not some fly-by-night operator trying to sell you a magical system for beating the casinos. I believe in the results of this study, play the game on a regular basis based on the principles that I advocate, and put my reputation and my money where my mouth is!

# Chapter Two
# INITIAL RESEARCH

I hadn't planned to study different types of betting systems or write this book until two book reviews perked my interest. Both were written about my book, *The Ultimate Blackjack Book,* and both made mention of a small portion of this book that explained progressive betting. Frank Scoblete, best-selling author of numerous books about casino gambling, said, "Thomason's prescription for winning is therefore radically different from my own and other experts who fully buy into the card counting credo. . . . I also believe that many of the traditional blackjack writers will mount Thomason's picture on their walls and throw darts at it for daring to challenge their orthodoxy and enter their domain." John Grochowski, author and syndicated columnist for the *Chicago Sun-Times*, said, ". . . progressions can turn some sessions from winners into losers. Losses after winning hands come with larger bets on the table. These take their toll and in the long run cancel out short-term gains from the progression." Both reviewers recommended the book to their readers, but both obviously weren't comfortable with my stand on progressive betting.

Although most books about blackjack seldom mention progressive betting in a positive manner, I wasn't aware that my advice was either questionable or controversial. On numerous occasions I'd discussed my chosen playing method with my colleagues, who stated that they believed system betting of any type was ineffectual, but that they had no strong foundation for believing so. They simply felt that card counting was the only sure way to have a shot at long-term profits. Several were convinced that computer analysis of progressive betting schemes must have been done, but none were able to put their hands on any published studies. The standard response to my question, "Why hasn't progressive betting been compared to card counting or flat betting?" was always the same: "There's no reason to, because progressive betting doesn't work."

One of my readers sent me information that led to my discovery of a brief mention of progressive betting. In his book, *Professional Blackjack* (PiYee Press, 1994) Stanford Wong attempts to totally discount writers who propose progressive betting systems. He states, "Common sense seems to support the notion that there are runs of good and bad luck . . . What seems to be common sense sometimes is nonsense."

He then presents a study which shows that winning streaks are as likely to occur as losing streaks. He concludes that there is absolutely no relationship between the win, loss, or push results of a hand based on the results of the two previous hands, and ends with the observation that, "streaks occur, but they cannot be predicted."

It's my opinion that Mr. Wong's study is irrelevant, and that he doesn't fully understand my approach to progressive betting. I'll explain my position at the conclusion of this book.

Unquestionably, the gauntlet had been thrown; the challenge to my beliefs had been made. Even though my professional associates respected the quality of my literary style and felt that my book was "A useful contribution to every player's library," they doubted the accuracy of my advice about progressive betting.

Since I was unable to locate any comparative studies on the subject, my next thought was that there must be computer software capable of analyzing the differences between betting styles, computer programs that could analyze and print out the results of millions of hands of consecutive play and compare the relative merits of the different types of betting systems available.

I was wrong. After purchasing two of the leading software programs, I discovered that progressive betting was never taken into consideration when the programs were designed! Computer programs allow the user to compare various types of card counting systems with different game rules or with a flat betting system that employs Basic Strategy play. That's it!

In spite of several books about progressive betting that continue to be reprinted and sold to the general public, and in spite of the fact that millions of players use some type of progressive system, I was unable to locate any reputable author, statistician, or gaming expert who has conducted a comparative analysis of progressive betting, card counting, and flat betting. Considering that blackjack may be the most researched casino table game in the world, I found this revelation to be both surprising and disconcerting. How is it possible that one of the most popular forms of blackjack betting could be ignored by those who profess to want to improve the players' chances of winning?

These initial findings — or lack of findings — encouraged me to pursue the issue. Why have the computer experts not created programs which compare progressive betting to other systems of play?

Letters to two gaming statisticians received no response. A telephone conversation with one of the programmers of a best-selling software package resulted in the following response to the question previously asked of my colleagues: "There's no reason to, because progressive systems don't work." He also told me it was impossible to modify his software to serve my purpose.

I contacted two computer programmers in my local area, explained my problem, and requested a quote as to how much it would cost to alter an existing program or create a new one that would help me with my study. Both estimates came in at over $7,000, with the likelihood that the cost would be higher. Frankly, I couldn't afford this expenditure. Contrary to popular belief, writers of casino gaming books don't make a heck of a lot of money!

At this point I decided to abandon my search for existing sources of information and do the research myself — manually, without the aid of computer-generated data.

My first study was a simple comparison of flat betting and progressive betting. Over 2,300 bets were made by two players, one using a progressive system and one betting the same amount each time — both playing *the exact same hands*. Each player lost 52.5% of his wagers and won 47.5% of his wagers — close to normal expectation for this game.

I was pleased by the results of this study, because, although both players lost money, the progressive player lost *less* than the flat bettor. This indicated the possibility that the experts could be wrong in assuming that there is no possible long-term difference between flat betting and progressive betting.

About the same time I was working on this initial research, I read an advertisement for a new blackjack book by Fred Renzey, entitled *The Blackjack Bluebook*. I ordered his book for two reasons: I read everything I can find on the game, plus one of the chapter headings was "Why Progressive Systems Don't Work." After reading the book (which is one of the best I've ever read about the game) I wrote Fred a lengthy letter responding to his "anti-progressive" arguments. This lead to several hour-long telephone conversations in which we presented our respective positions on the issue, and eventually our mutual efforts to analyze the merits of progressive betting. Fred, due to his analytical and mathematical background, was somewhat of a "devil's advocate," offsetting my personal prejudices in favor of progressive systems.

Fred's first analytical contribution to our investigation was a 792-hand simulation comparing a card counting system to a progressive betting system. After 792 hands, the counter was losing $1,742, primarily due to an unusually high percentage of losing hands while the count was very positive and larger wagers were on the table. The progressive bettor was losing $1,235 — not as much as the counter, but not supportive of the value of this betting system. An analysis of the 792 hands revealed that the percentage of consecutive wins compared to the percentage of consecutive losses was out of line with long-term probability. There were 21 "runs," or clusters, of consecutive winning hands of four or more, and 27 runs of consecutive losses of four or more. Of the 48 runs of wins or losses, 43% were clusters of consecutive wins — a lower percentage than would be expected over a long period of play, and the primary reason for the progressive bettor's losses.

Obviously the sample we were using — 792 hands — was too small to yield results that could be applied to long-term expectation.

This study also revealed several other problems which prevented a fair comparison of the three betting systems:

1. Fred was using a highly sophisticated counting system that only an advanced card counter could understand or apply.

2. Fred's counting system required as many as 48 possible changes in Basic Strategy based on the count — changes that the progressive bettor would never make. Consequently the progressive bettor and the flat bettor would not be playing the same hands in the same way.

3. The "surrender rule" that Fred applied was based on the count, and the times when surrender is appropriate are different for the card counter and the progressive or flat bettors.

It became clear that we had to develop a more simplified and equitable "playing field," both for the benefit of our readers and the integrity of the study.

After several months of groundwork, we developed a "Game Plan" to conduct a comprehensive study, which is explained in the next chapter.

# Chapter Three
# GROUND RULES

After several weeks of discussion and debate, Fred and I agreed on a number of principles that would set the stage for our analytical comparison. The guidelines were as follows:

1. "Keep it simple, stupid!" We wanted the study to be comprehensible and useful to the average blackjack player: No complicated algebraic formulas, no advanced statistical computation — just plain old addition, subtraction, multiplication, and division. Anyone with a fifth grade education should be able to understand, verify, and/or duplicate our study.

2. Each of the different types of players — the flat bettor, the progressive bettor, and the card counter — would play the same exact hands in the same exact way in exactly the same order. These would be our constants. The only difference between players — the only variable — would be the amount they bet on each hand. The card counter, using his betting system, would play and record the win, loss, and tie results for each hand. The flat bettor would use the same results and apply his betting system to them. Then the progressive bettor would take the same results and apply his betting system to them.

3. All three players would use the same Basic Strategy. The decisions to stand, hit, split, or double-down would be based on pre-established Basic Strategy guidelines (presented later in this

chapter), and the win, loss, and push results would be identical for all three players.

4. All hands would be manually dealt, without use of computer software or computer analysis. As previously stated, we could locate no computer programs capable of conducting this comparison, so we really had no other option but to deal the game manually. Also, many readers are not computer literate and might have problems interpreting or reproducing our work.

5. The rules of the game would be identical for all three types of bettors, and would be similar to those commonly found in most casinos. For instance, it would be foolish to study a single-deck game where the dealer dealt all of the cards before reshuffling. As advantageous as this might be to an expert card counter, it's a game condition that is rarely (if ever) found in today's casinos.

6. For the sake of accuracy and speed, the game would be a head-to-head match between the dealer and one player, acting on behalf of all three bettors. This would also reduce the chance of making card counting errors since there would be fewer cards to evaluate on each hand.

7. For the sake of accuracy, the hands would be dealt *very slowly,* Basic Strategy decisions would be constantly reviewed, and all compilations and computations would be checked and rechecked.

8. A very basic type of counting system and very basic type of progressive betting system would be employed. This would make it easier to conduct the study and easier to interpret the results.

Once we established the overall conditions that would govern our comparison, we agreed upon the following game rules and conditions and method of play:

# METHOD OF PLAY

The game would be dealt from a "shoe" using six decks, since six-deck games are the most common in today's casinos.

Five of six decks would be dealt from each shoe, providing approximately 83.3% penetration (exposure of 83.3% of the cards). This penetration level is considered excellent for the card counter because it theoretically allows more opportunities to take advantage of high counts.

A standard "Las Vegas style" shuffle would be used before the start of each shoe. The remainder of the deck would be "plugged" into the discard stack. The discard stack would be split in half and plugged in a criss-cross manner, then split into two equal stacks. The cards would then be intermingled using "triple rifs" of approximately one deck each, then a "single rif" of one deck each. The full six decks would then be cut by the player and the cut card positioned between the fifth and sixth deck of the shoe. Prior to dealing, the first card out of the shoe is displayed to the player and then discarded. Once the cut card is reached in the shoe, the hand in play is completed and the cards are reshuffled prior to the start of the next shoe. The shuffling method just described is the most common currently used in American casinos.

One exception to normal playing conditions is that the player is allowed all the time he wants to consider playing or betting options. The dealer only deals when the player is totally convinced that his betting decision, strategy decision, or card counting accuracy is correct. There are no fast dealers or other distractions that normally plague the black-jack player!

# RULES OF PLAY

**Dealer:**
Must hit 16 and stand on any 17.
Pays 3 to 2 for Blackjack.
Checks for Blackjack prior to dealing to the player.
Deals all player cards face up.
Deals his first card face down and any other cards face up.

**Player:**
Can split any pair. Only one card allowed on split aces.
Can re-split up to four hands.
Can double-down on any two cards.
Can double-down after splitting.
Never takes insurance.*
The "surrender" option is not available.*

* The insurance and surrender options have been excluded from this game because the use of these options by the card counter is considerably different than the use of these options by a flat or progressive bettor, and would cause the card counter to alter basic strategy more often than the flat or progressive bettor.

With the exception of lack of surrender, and the refusal to take insurance (which usually favors the casino anyway), the game rules presented are favorable to the players and are common to most casinos.

# BASIC STRATEGY

The basic strategy identically employed by all three types of players is as follows:

## BLACKJACK
## MULTIPLE DECK BASIC STRATEGY

Henry Tamburin
Research Services Unltd.

### PLAYER'S HAND VS. DEALER'S HAND

### HARD HANDS

| Player's Hand | | |
|---|---|---|
| 8 | Always Hit | |
| 9 | Double vs. 3–6 | Otherwise Hit |
| 10 | Double vs. 2–9 | Hit vs. 10, Ace |
| 11 | Double vs. 2–10 | Hit vs. Ace |
| 12 | Stand vs. 4–6 | Otherwise Hit |
| 13–16 | Stand vs. 2–6 | Otherwise Hit |
| 17–21 | Always Stand | |

### SOFT HANDS

| | | |
|---|---|---|
| A,2; A,3 | Double vs. 5–6 | Otherwise Hit |
| A,4; A,5 | Double vs. 4–6 | Otherwise Hit |
| A,6 | Double vs. 3–6 | Otherwise Hit |
| A,7 | Double vs. 3–6, Hit vs. 9, 10, Ace | Otherwise Stand |
| A,8; A,9 | Always Stand | |

15

## PAIRS

| | | |
|---|---|---|
| 2,2 | Split vs. 2–7 | Otherwise Hit |
| 3,3 | Split vs. 2–7 | Otherwise Hit |
| 4,4 | Split vs. 5–6 | Otherwise Hit |
| 5,5 | Double vs. 2–9 | Hit vs. 10–Ace |
| 6,6 | Split vs. 2–6 | Otherwise Hit |
| 7,7 | Split vs. 2–7 | Otherwise Hit |
| 8,8 | Always Split | |
| 9,9 | Split vs. 2–6, 8, 9 | Otherwise Stand |
| 10,10 | Always Stand | |
| A,A | Always Split | |

Note: Dealer stands on Soft 17. Double-Down after pair splitting allowed.

Most gaming experts agree that this strategy is the best one to use for the type of game described above.


# PLAYER BETTING RULES

Since all three players will be playing the same cards by the same rules and by the same basic strategy, the only factor that distinguishes them from one another is *how much they wager on each hand*. All other factors are identical. The rationale and amounts wagered are different for each player, based on the type of player they are — card counter, progressive bettor, or flat bettor. The only thing they have in common is that their initial bet on the first hand of a new shoe is the same amount for each player. In this comparative study, the initial bet at the start of the shoe for each type of player is $20.

16

How the players handle their bankroll after making this initial wager is the core of this analysis.

Each player must follow his own prescribed pattern of betting, without change or variation of any kind. In other words, the card counter must increase or decrease his bet as directed by his count chart, the progressive bettor must increase or decrease his bet as directed by his progressive betting rules, and the flat bettor must never increase or decrease his initial $20 bet, as dictated by his chosen wagering plan.

Logically, the player with the largest profit (or smallest loss) may have a betting plan superior to that of the other two players, since this is the *only* variable in the game.

The betting systems used by each type of player are as follows:

Flat bettor: Wagers $20 on each bet.

Progressive bettor: Wagers $20 as an initial bet on each hand, increases the starting bet by $10 each time he is a net winner on a hand, and decreases the bet to $20 when he is a net loser on a hand. He "caps off" his bet increases when he reaches a single bet of $50.

For example, if the player were to have net winning bets on six consecutive hands, his initial bets on each hand would have been $20, then $30, $40, $50, $50, and $50, in that order.

Had he netted a profit on two hands, then lost two hands, then won two hands, his betting pattern would have been $20, $30, $40, $20, $20, $30, because he increased his bet after a win and decreased to the original bet after a loss.

Also, if the progressive bettor won more than one bet on a hand due to favorable splits or double-downs, his increase on the next hand would

17

still remain at $10. If he "pushed" a hand (tied the dealer) or won one half of a split while losing the other half, resulting in a tie, the amount of the bet on the next hand would remain the same as the bet on the hand that pushed or tied.

The progressive bettor must revert to the initial $20 bet at the start of a new shoe, regardless of where he was in the progression.

Winning blackjack hands count as a single wager win, so if the progressive bettor is at the $30 level and draws a winning blackjack, he only increases his bet by $10 on the next hand.

Card Counter: The card counter uses the Black Ace Count Strategy (for four or six decks), a simple counting system developed by Fred Renzey and described in *Blackjack Bluebook*. The card rankings for this system are as follows:

| | |
|---|---|
| 2 = 0 | 9 = 0 |
| 3 = +1 | 10 = 0 |
| 4 = +1 | J = –1 |
| 5 = +1 | Q = –1 |
| 6 = +1 | K = –1 |
| 7 = 0 | Red A = 0 |
| 8 = 0 | Black A = –1 |

Simply stated, a count of +1 is assigned to 3 through 6, and a count of –1 is assigned to face cards and the black aces.

Each new shoe begins with a count of +8, and the bet is increased once the running count reaches +20 or more.

The running count and the betting strategy are as follows:

Through 19 — Bet one unit ($20)

Twenty or twenty-one — Bet three units ($60)

Twenty-two — Bet six units ($120)

Twenty-three — Bet eight units ($160)

Twenty-four or higher — Bet 12 units ($240)

According to Fred, this counting method carries an 86% efficiency rating for monitoring where the advantage lies. In computer simulation runs, it improved the player's performance by about 1% over basic strategy in typical blackjack games, providing him with an overall advantage of approximately one-half percent — just about as effective as more advanced systems but much easier for an inexperienced player to learn and apply.

So there you have it: The basic playing rules, the basic game rules, and the basic strategy and wagering rules. If you don't understand these rules and strategies, it might be wise to review a "basics" blackjack book, such as my *Blackjack for the Clueless,* or *Best Blackjack* by Frank Scoblete.

Now it's time to play the game!

# Chapter Four
# PLAYING THE GAME

Our next task was to play enough hands of blackjack, using the previously established rules and conditions, to be able to compare the three distinctly different betting systems.

I created a chart to record the results of play on each hand, which illustrates the total number of bets won, lost, or pushed by all three bettors at the conclusion of each shoe. Explanations of the chart and the results of play for one shoe are illustrated in the next chapter.

Traditionally, blackjack simulations have been specially designed computer software programs totally dedicated to card counting systems, and have presented the result of millions of hands of play. As previously stated, traditional methods of analysis could not be applied to our research because the sequential nature of progressive betting could not be tabulated by using computer-generated data.

I pondered the question, "How many shoes would have to be played to allow a fair comparison of the three systems?" Obviously a million-hand simulation was impractical. With practice, it took me about 40 minutes to deal the hands and record the results for one shoe. I averaged about 50 hands per shoe, so it took me approximately 10 and one-third hours to deal and record 1,000 hands of play. To play 10,000 hands would take over 103 hours. To play 100,000 hands would take 1,033 hours, and to play a million hands would take 10,330 hours — over 430 days if I played non-stop for 24 hours a day. I enjoy playing blackjack, but not *that* much!

I contacted other casino gaming experts regarding the size of our sample simulation — the number of hands that should be played to provide reliable data — but received no definitive answer because to the best of their knowledge no one had ever attempted this type of comparative study. Consequently, I chose to deal and record completed shoes until definite and sustained patterns became obvious.

I dealt and recorded the results of play for every hand, and tabulated the outcome for each shoe. After 2,000 hands, a pattern — a difference between the three types of betting systems — began to emerge. After 3,000 hands the pattern was essentially the same. To insure the probability that the pattern would remain consistent, I decided to enlarge the study to 5,000 hands of play, and then draw conclusions from this sample.

How long would it take the average blackjack player to play 5,000 hands? Most experts agree that casino blackjack under normal conditions averages around 80 hands per hour, and that the average player plays about four hours (320 hands) per day. Based on these numbers, 5,000 hands of blackjack would take about 15 and one-half days to play — equivalent to several three to four day trips to Las Vegas, Atlantic City, or other gaming meccas.

Critics may claim that 5,000 hands are too few upon which to draw reliable conclusions. I disagree and believe that 5,000 hands, as applied to the parameters of this study, provide a large enough sample to project predictable long-term results of play. I also believe that 5,000 hands are sufficient to make viable comparisons of the three betting systems under consideration.

For the next few chapters we'll add up the numbers and compare the different betting systems. Die-hard traditionalists will be surprised by the findings.

# Chapter Five
# METHOD OF RECORDING
# RESULTS OF PLAY

A special form was designed to record the results of each hand of play.

An illustration of a completed shoe (Shoe #2) is presented on the following page.

An explanation of each column, from left to right, is as follows:

1. Hand #: Shoe #2 began with the 50th hand dealt and ended with the 98th hand dealt. All hands, from one to 5,000, were dealt in consecutive order.

2. After Play Count: Each new shoe began with an assigned count of +8, as required by Renzey's Black Ace Count system. During the dealing of Hand #50, cards were exposed that resulted in a count of –2 for the hand. This negative count was subtracted from the initial count of +8, leaving a running count of +6 for the start of Hand #51. The running count was calculated for each hand, and justified the bet increases or decreases made by the card counter.

3. Win/Loss: These two columns list the bets won or lost on each hand. If two or more wins or two or more losses are listed in the same column, this indicates that the player split and/or doubled his hand in accordance with Basic Strategy guidelines.

For example, on Hand #69 the player dou-

| Hand # | After Play Count | Win | Loss | Push | Split | Double | Blackjack | Counter Units Bet | Counter Running Total | Prog Running Total |
|---|---|---|---|---|---|---|---|---|---|---|
| 50 | 8 | | L | | | | DEALER | 1 | –1 | –20 |
| 51 | 6 | W | | | | | | 1 | 0 | 0 |
| 52 | 3 | W | | | | | | 1 | 1 | 30 |
| 53 | 4 | W | | | | | | 1 | 2 | 70 |
| 54 | 5 | W | | | | | | 1 | 3 | 120 |
| 55 | 3 | W | | | | | | 1 | 4 | 170 |
| 56 | 5 | | L | | | | | 1 | 3 | 120 |
| 57 | 3 | W | | | | | PLAYER | 1 | 4(1/2) | 150 |
| 58 | 4 | W | | | | | | 1 | 5 | 180 |
| 59 | 6 | | | P | | | | 1 | 5 | 180 |
| 60 | 7 | W | | | | | | 1 | 6 | 220 |
| 61 | 9 | | L | | | | | 1 | 5 | 170 |
| 62 | 8 | | L | | | | | 1 | 4 | 150 |
| 63 | 8 | | L | | | | DEALER | 1 | 3 | 130 |
| 64 | 8 | W | | | | | | 1 | 4 | 150 |
| 65 | 11 | | | P | | | | 1 | 4 | 150 |
| 66 | 10 | W | | | | | PLAYER | 1 | 5(1/2) | 195 |
| 67 | 7 | | | P | | | | 1 | 5 | 195 |
| 68 | 7 | W | | | | | | 1 | 6 | 235 |
| 69 | 11 | W/W | | | | D | | 2 | 8 | 335 |
| 70 | 9 | W | | | | | | 1 | 9 | 385 |
| 71 | 10 | | L | | | | | 1 | 8 | 335 |
| 72 | 10 | | | P | | | | 1 | 8 | 335 |
| 73 | 12 | | L | | | | | 1 | 7 | 315 |

| Hand | Count | W | L | P | S | D | PLAYER / DEALER | Units | ± | Total |
|---|---|---|---|---|---|---|---|---|---|---|
| 74 | 12 | | L | | | | | 1 | 6 | 295 |
| 75 | 12 | W | | | | | | 1 | 7 | 315 |
| 76 | 10 | | L | | | | | 1 | 6 | 285 |
| 77 | 9 | W | | | | | | 1 | 7(1/2) | 315 |
| 78 | 8 | | L | | | | | 1 | 6 | 285 |
| 79 | 7 | W | | | | | | 1 | 7 | 305 |
| 80 | 9 | | L | | | | | 1 | 6 | 275 |
| 81 | 8 | W | | | | | | 1 | 7 | 295 |
| 82 | 8 | | L | | | | | 1 | 6 | 265 |
| 83 | 11 | | L | | | | | 1 | 5 | 245 |
| 84 | 12 | | L | | S | | | 1 | 4 | 225 |
| Q85 | 9 | | LLL | P | | | PLAYER | 1 | 3 | 215 |
| 86 | 8 | | L | | | D | | 3 | 2 | 185 |
| 87 | 12 | | L | | | D | | 1 | -1 | 125 |
| 88 | 8 | WW | | | | | | 2 | -1 | 125 |
| 89 | 9 | W | | | | | | 1 | 1 | 165 |
| 90 | 7 | W | | | | | | 1 | -2 | 195 |
| 91 | 5 | W | | | | | | 1 | 3 | 235 |
| 92 | 5 | | L | | | | DEALER | 1 | 4 | 285 |
| 93 | 9 | | | | | | | 1 | 3 | 235 |
| 94 | 10 | W | LL | | | D | | 2 | 4 | 255 |
| 95 | 10 | WW | L | P | | D | | 2 | 6 | 315 |
| 96 | 10 | | | | | | | 1 | 4 | 235 |
| 97 | 13 | | | | | | | 1 | 3 | 215 |
| 98 | 14 | | | | | | | | 3 | 215 |
| END SHOE2 | | 26 | 23 | 6 | 1 | 5 | 6 | | $90 | $215 |

27

bled on the hand and won both wagers. On Hand #87 the player split the hand, doubled on one of the splits, and lost both hands to a superior dealer hand. This caused a loss of three bets — the original bet, the matching split bet, and the double-down bet.

4. Push: A push was recorded when the dealer and player tied and no money changed hands.

5. Split/Double: The next two columns show when the player split and/or doubled on a hand, and explain why the player increased his bet.

6. Blackjack: This column records dealer or player blackjacks.

7. Counter Units Bet: This column lists the units bet by the card counter. One unit is equal to $20. The unit designation was used rather than the dollar designation in order to simplify recording the one to 12 unit bet spread used by the counter.

8. Counter Running Total: This column shows the running total of units won or lost by the card counter at the conclusion of each hand.

For example, at the conclusion of Hand #56, the card counter was three units ($60) ahead. He won Hand #57 with a blackjack, received a payment of one and one-half units (3 to 2 on blackjack) and concluded this hand with a running profit of four and one-half units. Note: To make the math simpler the one-half unit wins are not included in the running count, but are added to the total at the end of the shoe.

9. Progressive Running Total: This column records the running totals for the progressive bettor using the $20 to $50 bet spread previously explained.

For example, the progressive player lost

Hand #50 to the dealer's blackjack and ended up a $20 loser. His next bet (Hand #51) was $20, since he lost the previous hand. He won this bet and had a running total of $-0- . Since he showed a net profit on Hand #51, his initial bet for Hand #52 was $30. He won Hand #52, and concluded with a net running profit of $30. He increased his bet to $40 on Hand #54, won the hand, and ended with a running profit of $70.

Running totals were recorded at the end of each hand, and the progressive bettor showed a net profit of $215 when the shoe ended with Hand #98.

10. Totals: The totals for each column are displayed at the end of the shoe. Only the Counter Running Total column requires explanation: The $90 result was calculated by multiplying the running units for the final hand of the shoe — 3 — by $20, then adding the one-half units won during the course of the shoe — a total of three (3) one-half units. In other words, $3 \times \$20 + 3 \times \$10 = \$90$.

We had originally planned to include in this book the hand-by-hand results for all 102 shoes. This 5,000-hand list could be used by players to compare their personal betting system to the systems used by the authors.

Unfortunately, the inclusion of all of the completed shoes would have added another 200 pages to the manuscript and doubled the retail price of the book. The costs seemed prohibitive since the majority of readers would not choose to run comparative analyses.

The 102 shoes are available to interested parties by contacting me at the address listed at the end of the book.

# Chapter Six
# OVERALL RESULTS

The card counter, the flat bettor, and the progressive bettor all experienced the same wins, losses, pushes, and blackjacks for the 102 shoes of play. I hate to keep emphasizing this fact, but the only difference in their profits or losses was how much they chose to wager on each hand. The amount they wagered and the amount they won or lost will be presented in later chapters of this book.

The following chart illustrates the end-of-shoe results for all 102 shoes played:

## Summary of 102 Shoes of Play:
## Wins, Losses, Pushes, and Blackjacks

| Shoe # | Wins | Losses | Pushes | Blackjacks Player | Dealer |
|--------|------|--------|--------|--------|--------|
| 1. | 26 | 27 | 1 | 5 | 1 |
| 2. | 26 | 23 | 6 | 3 | 3 |
| 3. | 25 | 30 | 4 | 2 | 2 |
| 4. | 28 | 23 | 6 | 1 | 3 |
| 5. | 19 | 28 | 6 | 1 | 3 |
| 6. | 22 | 28 | 4 | 4 | 3 |
| 7. | 24 | 26 | 2 | 5 | 0 |
| 8. | 27 | 27 | 2 | 0 | 2 |
| 9. | 22 | 27 | 6 | 3 | 1 |
| 10. | 29 | 21 | 4 | 4 | 0 |
| 11. | 23 | 31 | 3 | 3 | 4 |
| 12. | 25 | 23 | 7 | 2 | 3 |
| 13. | 23 | 27 | 0 | 3 | 1 |
| 14. | 23 | 29 | 3 | 2 | 0 |

| Shoe # | Wins | Losses | Pushes | Blackjacks | |
|--------|------|--------|--------|--------|--------|
| | | | | Player | Dealer |
| 15. | 28 | 24 | 4 | 0 | 2 |
| 16. | 25 | 27 | 3 | 0 | 4 |
| 17. | 20 | 31 | 5 | 3 | 2 |
| 18. | 21 | 27 | 9 | 3 | 3 |
| 19. | 24 | 30 | 4 | 1 | 2 |
| 20. | 27 | 20 | 5 | 2 | 3 |
| 21. | 28 | 22 | 5 | 3 | 0 |
| 22. | 28 | 22 | 5 | 4 | 3 |
| 23. | 19 | 35 | 6 | 3 | 3 |
| 24. | 18 | 32 | 1 | 2 | 0 |
| 25. | 26 | 28 | 0 | 5 | 3 |
| 26. | 28 | 20 | 7 | 3 | 0 |
| 27. | 19 | 31 | 4 | 3 | 4 |
| 28. | 26 | 25 | 3 | 3 | 4 |
| 29. | 23 | 24 | 9 | 1 | 2 |
| 30. | 22 | 32 | 4 | 1 | 5 |
| 31. | 26 | 18 | 8 | 3 | 3 |
| 32. | 24 | 26 | 7 | 1 | 1 |
| 33. | 25 | 26 | 1 | 4 | 1 |
| 34. | 20 | 32 | 5 | 3 | 2 |
| 35. | 27 | 19 | 6 | 1 | 2 |
| 36. | 17 | 33 | 9 | 1 | 3 |
| 37. | 27 | 30 | 7 | 3 | 0 |
| 38. | 30 | 23 | 5 | 2 | 0 |
| 39. | 29 | 22 | 4 | 3 | 1 |
| 40. | 27 | 20 | 7 | 1 | 2 |
| 41. | 32 | 21 | 3 | 3 | 0 |
| 42. | 22 | 24 | 4 | 1 | 2 |
| 43. | 22 | 27 | 5 | 2 | 1 |
| 44. | 25 | 27 | 4 | 1 | 4 |
| 45. | 17 | 28 | 10 | 2 | 0 |
| 46. | 28 | 19 | 5 | 1 | 1 |
| 47. | 22 | 32 | 4 | 1 | 2 |
| 48. | 22 | 26 | 7 | 2 | 3 |
| 49. | 34 | 17 | 4 | 5 | 1 |
| 50. | 20 | 30 | 3 | 3 | 2 |

| Shoe # | Wins | Losses | Pushes | Blackjacks | |
| --- | --- | --- | --- | --- | --- |
| | | | | Player | Dealer |
| 51. | 22 | 33 | 4 | 3 | 3 |
| 52. | 29 | 27 | 3 | 1 | 3 |
| 53. | 28 | 22 | 3 | 4 | 0 |
| 54. | 24 | 32 | 3 | 1 | 2 |
| 55. | 27 | 24 | 5 | 2 | 3 |
| 56. | 29 | 22 | 5 | 4 | 3 |
| 57. | 29 | 26 | 3 | 4 | 2 |
| 58. | 28 | 24 | 4 | 2 | 4 |
| 59. | 22 | 33 | 1 | 2 | 1 |
| 60. | 25 | 24 | 5 | 4 | 1 |
| 61. | 26 | 22 | 6 | 3 | 2 |
| 62. | 27 | 27 | 2 | 3 | 2 |
| 63. | 23 | 25 | 4 | 1 | 3 |
| 64. | 16 | 32 | 9 | 0 | 5 |
| 65. | 17 | 28 | 9 | 2 | 5 |
| 66. | 22 | 24 | 7 | 1 | 4 |
| 67. | 24 | 26 | 5 | 5 | 1 |
| 68. | 25 | 25 | 3 | 1 | 3 |
| 69. | 21 | 29 | 6 | 2 | 2 |
| 70. | 22 | 30 | 5 | 3 | 1 |
| 71. | 24 | 35 | 1 | 1 | 4 |
| 72. | 20 | 25 | 6 | 3 | 1 |
| 73. | 26 | 29 | 2 | 1 | 2 |
| 74. | 29 | 24 | 5 | 1 | 3 |
| 75. | 29 | 22 | 5 | 5 | 2 |
| 76. | 29 | 23 | 4 | 4 | 0 |
| 77. | 26 | 20 | 6 | 4 | 3 |
| 78. | 28 | 21 | 5 | 3 | 2 |
| 79. | 19 | 32 | 6 | 4 | 0 |
| 80. | 23 | 28 | 5 | 2 | 3 |
| 81. | 28 | 25 | 5 | 4 | 1 |
| 82. | 29 | 23 | 2 | 2 | 3 |
| 83. | 24 | 27 | 4 | 4 | 3 |
| 84. | 28 | 24 | 3 | 3 | 3 |
| 85. | 30 | 22 | 3 | 3 | 0 |
| 86. | 30 | 25 | 3 | 0 | 1 |

| | | | | Blackjacks | |
|:---:|:---:|:---:|:---:|:---:|:---:|
| **Shoe #** | **Wins** | **Losses** | **Pushes** | **Player** | **Dealer** |
| 87. | 19 | 29 | 8 | 3 | 3 |
| 88. | 26 | 22 | 7 | 3 | 0 |
| 89. | 23 | 29 | 2 | 1 | 3 |
| 90. | 23 | 29 | 3 | 1 | 1 |
| 91. | 29 | 18 | 7 | 4 | 1 |
| 92. | 28 | 26 | 4 | 4 | 1 |
| 93. | 26 | 20 | 8 | 2 | 2 |
| 94. | 28 | 24 | 5 | 5 | 2 |
| 95. | 25 | 31 | 23 | 1 | 2 |
| 96. | 20 | 33 | 3 | 1 | 3 |
| 97. | 20 | 29 | 3 | 2 | 1 |
| 98. | 28 | 28 | 2 | 2 | 2 |
| 99. | 33 | 20 | 4 | 2 | 3 |
| 100. | 23 | 27 | 5 | 1 | 0 |
| 101. | 23 | 28 | 2 | 4 | 3 |
| 102. | 32 | 33 | 6 | 0 | 6 |
| Totals: | 2,534 (Wins) | 2,666 (Losses) | 464 (Pushes) | 245 (Player BJs) | 208 (Dealer BJs) |

Total number of wagers placed on 5,000 hands: 5,664.

| | |
|---|---|
| Wins: | 45% |
| Losses: | 47% |
| Pushes: | 8% |
| Total: | 100% |

As explained earlier, the results are compiled for win, loss, or push *bets*, rather than win, loss, or push *hands*. This distinction is important because the player will normally average 10–12% more bets placed than initial hands dealt, due to double-downs and splits.

For instance, suppose that a player was dealt

a pair of 7s and the dealer showed a 6 as his up-card. The correct Basic Strategy is to split the hand. After doing so, the player is dealt a 4 on the first 7, which calls for a double-down. The player draws a face card on the first half of the split and stands on 21. The dealer then deals to the second 7, and the player draws a 3 and correctly doubles his wager, draws a jack, and stands on 20.

In this example the player now has four bets riding on the original pair of 7s that were dealt to him. The dealer rolls over a face card as his bottom card, draws a queen, and busts with a total of 26 — just what we hoped would happen!

Consequently, the player won four separate wagers — four times the amount of the initial bet — as a result of the original hand dealt. Hands like these cause the 10 to 12% increase in bets made to hands played.

For our 5,000 hands of play, each player won 2,534 bets, lost 2,666 bets, pushed 464 bets, and drew 245 blackjacks from the 5,664 wagers placed on the table. This amounts to approximately 45% winning bets, 47% losing bets, and 8% pushes.

These percentages closely resemble the overall results of play for nine million hand computer-generated simulations, indicating that our 5,000 hands are a reliable sample of long-term expectation.

In the next few chapters we will analyze the difference in financial gain or loss to each type of bettor.

# Chapter Seven
# THREE-WAY COMPARISON
# OF BETTING STRATEGIES

Assuming that the 5,000 hands played are representative of the long term results of play (as was strongly indicated in the previous chapter), a three-way comparison based on money won or lost would indicate which type of betting system should be most profitable to the player.

The following chart illustrates how much money each type of player won and lost while following his preferred betting system. The win/loss results are summarized for each player at the end of each shoe, and the running total for each player is tabulated at the end of 102 shoes of play.

# THREE WAY COMPARISON
## TOTAL $ WON OR LOST PER SHOE

| SHOE # | FLAT BET | | PROGRESSIVE BET | | COUNTER BET | |
|---|---|---|---|---|---|---|
| | WIN | LOSS | WIN | LOSS | WIN | LOSS |
| 1. | $30 | | | $40 | $70 | |
| 2. | 90 | | $215 | | 90 | |
| 3. | | $80 | | 95 | | $580 |
| 4. | 110 | | 100 | | 110 | |
| 5. | | 170 | | 250 | | 210 |
| 6. | | 80 | | 90 | | 10 |
| 7. | 10 | | | 35 | 10 | |
| 8. | -0- | -0- | 40 | | -0- | -0- |
| 9. | | 70 | | 165 | 290 | |
| 10. | 200 | | 230 | | 200 | |
| 11. | | 130 | | 215 | 130 | |
| 12. | 60 | | 65 | | 20 | |
| 13. | | 50 | | 115 | 1,110 | |
| 14. | | 100 | | 150 | | 100 |
| 15. | 80 | | 40 | | 200 | |
| 16. | | 40 | | 120 | -0- | -0- |
| 17. | | 190 | | 135 | | 190 |
| 18. | | 90 | | 250 | | 50 |
| 19. | | 110 | 175 | | | 150 |
| 20. | 160 | | 360 | | 160 | |
| 21. | 150 | | 390 | | 150 | |
| 22. | 160 | | 175 | | 160 | |
| 23. | | 290 | | 260 | | 450 |
| 24. | | 260 | | 360 | | 260 |
| 25. | 10 | | | 90 | 10 | |
| 26. | 130 | | 320 | | 290 | |
| 27. | | 210 | | 140 | | 570 |
| 28. | 50 | | 95 | | | 450 |
| 29. | | 10 | | 100 | | 670 |
| 30. | | 190 | | 270 | | 160 |
| 31. | 190 | | 315 | | 190 | |
| 32. | | 30 | | 30 | | 30 |
| 33. | 20 | | 105 | | 280 | |
| 34. | | 210 | | 370 | | 290 |

| SHOE # | FLAT BET | | PROGRESSIVE BET | | COUNTER BET | |
|---|---|---|---|---|---|---|
| | WIN | LOSS | WIN | LOSS | WIN | LOSS |
| 35. | | $170 | $170 | | $130 | |
| 36. | | 340 | | 430 | | 2,060 |
| 37. | | 30 | | 190 | | 140 |
| 38. | 160 | | 105 | | 160 | |
| 39. | 170 | | 195 | | 170 | |
| 40. | 150 | | 305 | | 350 | |
| 41. | 250 | | 270 | | 330 | |
| 42. | | 20 | | 35 | 520 | |
| 43. | | 80 | | 60 | | 160 |
| 44. | | 30 | 100 | | | 30 |
| 45. | | 200 | | 160 | | 1,370 |
| 46. | 190 | | 400 | | 200 | |
| 47. | | 170 | | 170 | | 760 |
| 48. | | 20 | | 40 | | 20 |
| 49. | 390 | | 430 | | 1,280 | |
| 50. | | 190 | | 195 | | 170 |
| 51. | | 190 | | 360 | | 190 |
| 52. | 50 | | 30 | | | 120 |
| 53. | 160 | | 290 | | 460 | |
| 54. | | 150 | | 30 | | 150 |
| 55. | 80 | | | 5 | 80 | |
| 56. | 100 | | 240 | | -0- | -0- |
| 57. | 100 | | 75 | | 100 | |
| 58. | 100 | | 50 | | 100 | |
| 59. | | 200 | | 315 | | 200 |
| 60. | 60 | | | 65 | 60 | |
| 61. | 110 | | 175 | | 830 | |
| 62. | 30 | | 55 | | 550 | |
| 63. | | 30 | | 30 | | 30 |
| 64. | | 320 | | 440 | | 340 |
| 65. | | 200 | | 275 | | 200 |
| 66. | | 30 | | 70 | | 60 |
| 67. | | 10 | | 25 | 10 | |
| 68. | 10 | | | 25 | | 10 |
| 69. | | 140 | | 185 | | 140 |
| 70. | | 130 | | 160 | | 270 |
| 71. | | 210 | | 270 | | 210 |
| 72. | | 70 | | 100 | | 70 |

| SHOE # | FLAT BET | | PROGRESSIVE BET | | COUNTER BET | |
|---|---|---|---|---|---|---|
| | WIN | LOSS | WIN | LOSS | WIN | LOSS |
| 73. | | $50 | | $25 | | $50 |
| 74. | 110 | | 80 | | | 410 |
| 75. | 190 | | 215 | | 670 | |
| 76. | 160 | | 250 | | 160 | |
| 77. | 160 | | 195 | | 160 | |
| 78. | 170 | | 195 | | 210 | |
| 79. | | 220 | | 150 | | 20 |
| 80. | | 80 | | 85 | | 80 |
| 81. | 100 | | 230 | | 100 | |
| 82. | 150 | | 65 | | 150 | |
| 83. | -0- | -0- | 140 | | -0- | -0- |
| 84. | 110 | | 210 | | 730 | |
| 85. | 190 | | 280 | | 210 | |
| 86. | 100 | | 210 | | 100 | |
| 87. | | 170 | | 275 | | 370 |
| 88. | 110 | | 105 | | 110 | |
| 89. | | 110 | | 205 | | 110 |
| 90. | | 110 | | 150 | 500 | |
| 91. | 260 | | 405 | | 520 | |
| 92. | 80 | | | 40 | | 100 |
| 93. | 140 | | 300 | | 140 | |
| 94. | 130 | | | 10 | -0- | -0- |
| 95. | | 110 | | 250 | | 50 |
| 96. | | 250 | | 350 | | 270 |
| 97. | | 160 | | 125 | | 160 |
| 98. | 20 | | | 120 | 40 | |
| 99. | 280 | | | 475 | 460 | |
| 100. | | 70 | | 165 | | 550 |
| 101. | | 60 | | 105 | | 260 |
| 102. | | 20 | | 70 | | 40 |

TOTALS: $6,030 $6,640    $8,940 $8,970 $12,930 $13,470
W/L
Difference:          $-610        $ -30        $-540
Total of 5,000 hands played.

An analysis of the end-of-shoe results is as follows:

Flat Bettor: Won $6,030 Lost $6,640 Net loss of $610.

Card Counter: Won $12,930 Lost $13,470 Net loss of $540.

Progressive Bettor: Won $8,940 Lost $8,970 Net loss of $30.

How do these results compare to what is predicted by computer simulated play? The answer is somewhat obscure in two out of three cases:

1. Flat bettor: Most reputable casino gaming books tell us that the "Perfect Basic Strategy" player who bets the same initial amount of money on every hand faces a "house edge" of approximately one-half percent, depending on game rules. Financially speaking, this means that the flat bettor playing perfect basic strategy will lose, in the long run, 50 cents for every $100 wagered. In our 5,000 hand simulation our flat bettor wagered a total of $113,280 and lost $610 — about one-half percent *of the total amount wagered.*

Here's the rub: Many players don't understand that the player is subject to a one-half percent loss *for each and every bet placed.* In this case the flat bettor would be expected to lose ten cents each and every time he made a $20 bet. The flat bettor made 5,664 bets during the 5,000 hands of play, and theoretically should have lost $566.40 — pretty close to his actual loss of $610. Two or three bets made the difference between projected losses and actual losses.

2. Progressive bettor: Our progressive bettor was the only player to practically break even after 5,000 hands of play. Not impressive, but better than the other two players!

3. Card counter: Our card counter lost

$540. Is this relevant? Not necessarily, since card counters experience major "positive and negative fluctuations" during short-term play — and 5,000 hands is considered to be a very short term of play by proponents of this type of system. But according to the counting system being used in our study, the counter should average a 1% long term gain by counting cards, giving him a one-half percent advantage over the casino. The counter theoretically should have won one-half percent of the amount wagered on each hand.

It appears that the card counter experienced a "negative fluctuation" during the 5,000 hands of play.

So, in answer to one of the questions addressed in this study, the progressive bettor had better financial results than either the flat bettor or the card counter.

One of the weaknesses of some books about casino gaming is that the authors fail to provide the evidence to substantiate their claims — which is why you will have to suffer through the various charts included in this book.

I'm skeptical of writers who say, "I've conducted 976 studies of eight zillion hands of blackjack, and this is what I used to justify my claims." Unfortunately, we don't see the studies and we don't know how they were conducted.

I think you should have access to some of the raw data. If the numbers don't interest you, ignore them and only consider the totals presented at the conclusion of each chart.

Incidently, in a later chapter of this book entitled "Progressive Quit Points," I'll explain a playing tactic that would have made it possible for *all three of our players to have ended up winners.*

Meanwhile, the next chapter explains "running totals" and how they are influenced by the betting system that the player choses to employ.

# Chapter Eight
# RUNNING TOTALS

Blackjack is a game of ups and downs, peaks and valleys, wins and losses — a roller coaster ride that can make you rich and famous or broke and despondent. How you stand at any point in time during a session of play — up or down — can affect your overall attitude and your financial outcome. Consequently, your "running" results of play — how you stand at the conclusion of each shoe, for instance, is very important to most players.

The following chart illustrates the "running" total amount of money won or lost for each player at the conclusion of each consecutive shoe.

## RUNNING TOTALS

| SHOE# | FLAT BET | PROG. BET | COUNTER BET |
|:-----:|:--------:|:---------:|:-----------:|
| 1. | $+30 | $–40 | $+70 |
| 2. | +120 | +175 | +160 |
| 3. | +40 | +80 | –420 |
| 4. | +150 | +180 | –310 |
| 5. | –20 | –70 | –520 |
| 6. | –100 | –160 | –530 |
| 7. | –90 | –195 | –520 |
| 8. | –90 | –155 | –520 |
| 9. | –160 | –320 | –230 |
| 10. | +40 | –90 | –30 |
| 11. | –90 | –305 | –160 |
| 12. | –30 | –240 | –140 |

| SHOE# | FLAT BET | PROG. BET | COUNTER BET |
|-------|----------|-----------|-------------|
| 13. | –80 | –355 | +970 |
| 14. | –180 | –505 | +870 |
| 15. | –100 | –465 | +1,070 |
| 16. | –140 | –585 | +1,070 |
| 17. | –330 | –720 | +880 |
| 18. | –420 | –970 | +830 |
| 19. | –530 | –795 | +680 |
| 20. | –370 | –435 | +840 |
| 21. | –220 | –45 | +990 |
| 22. | –60 | +130 | +1,150 |
| 23. | –350 | –130 | +700 |
| 24. | –610 | –490 | +440 |
| 25. | –600 | –580 | +450 |
| 26. | –470 | –260 | +740 |
| 27. | –680 | –400 | +170 |
| 28. | –630 | –305 | –280 |
| 29. | –640 | –405 | –950 |
| 30. | –830 | –675 | –1,110 |
| 31. | –640 | –360 | –920 |
| 32. | –670 | –390 | –950 |
| 33. | –650 | –285 | –670 |
| 34. | –860 | –665 | –960 |
| 35. | –1,030 | –485 | –830 |
| 36. | –1,370 | –915 | –2,890 |
| 37. | –1,400 | –1105 | –3,030 |
| 38. | –1,240 | –1000 | –2,870 |
| 39. | –1,070 | –805 | –2,700 |
| 40. | –920 | –500 | –2,350 |
| 41. | –670 | –230 | –2,020 |
| 42. | –690 | –265 | –1,500 |
| 43. | –770 | –325 | –1,660 |
| 44. | –800 | –225 | –1,690 |
| 45. | –1,000 | –385 | –3,060 |
| 46. | –810 | +15 | –2,860 |
| 47. | –980 | –155 | –3,620 |
| 48. | –1,000 | –195 | –3,640 |

| SHOE# | FLAT BET | PROG. BET | COUNTER BET |
|-------|----------|-----------|-------------|
| 49. | –610 | +235 | –2,360 |
| 50. | –800 | +40 | –2,530 |
| 51. | –990 | –320 | –2,720 |
| 52. | –940 | –290 | –2,840 |
| 53. | –780 | –0– | –2,380 |
| 54. | –930 | –30 | –2,530 |
| 55. | –850 | –35 | –2,450 |
| 56. | –750 | +205 | –2,450 |
| 57. | –650 | +280 | –2,350 |
| 58. | –550 | +330 | –2,250 |
| 59. | –750 | +15 | –2,450 |
| 60. | –690 | –50 | –2,390 |
| 61. | –580 | +125 | –1,560 |
| 62. | –550 | +180 | –1,010 |
| 63. | –580 | +150 | –1,040 |
| 64. | –900 | –290 | –1,380 |
| 65. | –1,100 | –565 | –1,580 |
| 66. | –1,130 | –635 | –1,640 |
| 67. | –1,120 | –660 | –1,630 |
| 68. | –1,110 | –685 | –1,640 |
| 69. | –1,250 | –870 | –1,780 |
| 70. | –1,380 | –1030 | –2,050 |
| 71. | –1,590 | –1300 | –2,260 |
| 72. | –1,660 | –1400 | –2,330 |
| 73. | –1,710 | –1425 | –2,380 |
| 74. | –1,600 | –1345 | –2,790 |
| 75. | –1,410 | –1130 | –2,120 |
| 76. | –1,250 | –880 | –1,960 |
| 77. | –1,090 | –685 | –1,800 |
| 78. | –920 | –490 | –1,590 |
| 79. | –1,140 | –640 | –1,610 |
| 80. | –1,220 | –725 | –1,690 |
| 81. | –1,120 | –495 | –1,590 |
| 82. | –970 | –430 | –1,440 |
| 83. | –970 | –290 | –1,440 |
| 84. | –860 | –80 | –710 |

| SHOE# | FLAT BET | PROG. BET | COUNTER BET |
|-------|----------|-----------|-------------|
| 85. | −670 | +200 | −500 |
| 86. | −570 | +410 | −400 |
| 87. | −740 | +135 | −770 |
| 88. | −630 | +240 | −730 |
| 89. | −740 | +35 | −770 |
| 90. | −850 | −115 | −270 |
| 91. | −590 | +290 | +250 |
| 92. | −510 | +250 | +150 |
| 93. | −370 | +550 | +290 |
| 94. | −240 | +540 | +290 |
| 95. | −350 | +290 | +240 |
| 96. | −600 | −60 | −30 |
| 97. | −760 | −185 | −190 |
| 98. | −740 | −305 | −150 |
| 99. | −460 | +170 | +310 |
| 100. | −530 | +5 | −240 |
| 101. | −590 | −100 | −500 |
| 102. | −610 | −30 | −540 |

Number of times each type of bettor could have quit playing at the end of a shoe with some of the casino's money (a net profit for the session):

> Flat Bettor: 5
> Progressive Bettor: 26
> Counter Bettor: 23

Maximum bankroll required to survive losing periods:

> Flat Bettor: $1,710
> Progressive Bettor: $1,425
> Counter Bettor: $3,640

The following explanation will help you understand the chart:

The flat bettor won a total of $30 as a result of playing Shoe #1. He won $90 on the second shoe. The $90 profit plus the $30 profit on the first shoe gave him a running net profit of $120 after completing the first two shoes. He lost $80 on Shoe #3. Subtracting this amount from his previous net profit of $120 left him with a running net profit of $40 after three shoes of play.

The progressive bettor lost $40 on Shoe #1, but won $215 on Shoe #2, which gave him a net profit of $175 after two shoes of play. On the third shoe, he lost $95, for a total profit of $80 after three shoes.

The card counter won $70 on the first shoe and $90 on the second shoe, for a net profit of $160 after two shoes of play. On the third shoe he lost $580, for a net loss of $420 after three shoes of play.

The running total for each player was carried through to the completion of 102 shoes of play, and shows that the flat bettor ended up losing $610, the card counter ended up losing $540, and the progressive bettor ended up losing $30.

Two interesting questions can be answered by analyzing the shoe-by-shoe running totals.

The first question is, "How often was each type of player ahead of the casino?" Or stated differently, "How many times could each type of bettor have chosen to quit play at the end of a shoe with some of the casino's money in his pocket?"

The answer to the question is:

1. The flat bettor was ahead of the casino for five out of 102 shoes. There were only five opportunities for this player to quit the game in the plus

column — only about 5% of the time he was playing!

2. The card counter fared better: He had 23 opportunities to quit play as an overall winner — about 23% of the time he was playing. This also shows that he was losing money about 77% of the time.

3. The progressive bettor did better than the other two players. He was ahead of the casino at the end of 26 out of 102 shoes — about 27% of the time.

Obviously any player, regardless of his betting style, would rather be winning than losing. Our flat bettor seems to have never had a reasonable chance of quitting while ahead. He could have quit play after completing four shoes with a $150 profit. This amounted to around an hour's playing time — not long enough to satisfy the average player. In retrospect he should have quit, because by continuing to play he was losing by the end of the eleventh shoe and spent the next 91 shoes trying to realize a net profit and was unsuccessful in doing so. This is not my idea of a few fun days of recreational blackjack!

The card counter, on the other hand, experienced major fluctuations in wins and losses, and was substantially ahead of the casino on numerous occasions. Had he chosen to quit play at the end of Shoe #22 he could have left the tables with a profit of $1,150 — a pretty healthy amount of money! In a head-to-head game our players averaged around 50 hands per shoe, or around 1,100 hands for 22 shoes. Converting this to normal casino conditions, at an average of 80 hands per hour on a crowded table he would have played about 14 hours and averaged a profit of about $82 per hour. Not bad!

BUT, by continuing to play beyond Shoe #22, our card counter experienced many more losing shoes than winning shoes, lost all of his $1,150 in profits by the end of Shoe #28, and played the next 63 shoes with money from his own bankroll. He eventually reversed this pattern and was once again in the plus column at the end of Shoe #91. His recovery from serious losses could be considered a moral victory, but he still ended up losing after 5,000 hands of play.

The progressive bettor had a easier time at the tables, and could have quit play as a winner on more occasions than the card counter or the flat bettor. His high points in net profits ($410 at the end of Shoe #86 and $550 at the end of Shoe #93) were not as much as the card counter's high point, but his greatest number of consecutive shoes with a running loss was only 23. This compares to the card counter's negative running totals for 63 consecutive shoes and the flat bettor's negative running totals for 91 consecutive shoes.

Playing with the casino's money is obviously less stressful and more fun than risking your own bankroll. Even though winnings are *yours* the moment the chips cross the table, and are just as valuable as the money in your wallet, most players are more comfortable risking their profits than risking their original bankroll. Based on the patterns in our 5,000 hands of play, I'd much rather be the progressive bettor!

Speaking of bankrolls, the other question that can be answered by reviewing the running totals is, "How much of each player's bankroll was actually at risk during the 5,000 hands of play?" Stated differently, "How much cash would each type of bettor have had to invest in the game to survive losing periods?"

The answer to this question is determined by reviewing the running totals and seeing where each player stood at the peak of his losing period.

At one point, at the end of Shoe #73, the flat bettor was down $1,710. Consequently, he would have to have had a bankroll of $1,710 and have it all in the game in order to sustain these losses, plus enough money to place a bet on the first hand of the next shoe.

The card counter needed a much larger bankroll, for at the end of Shoe #48 his running losses totaled $3,640 — more than twice as much cash on the table as the flat bettor.

The progressive bettor's largest net loss was $1,425, which occurred at the end of Shoe #73. Consequently, the progressive bettor was able to play his game with a bankroll that was less than that required by the flat bettor, and much less than that required by the card counter.

And so, we can conclude that the progressive bettor was in the win column more often than the other two players, and risked a smaller amount of his cash than the other two players. Obviously, running totals reveal a lot about the game of blackjack.

The next chapter explains why our players won or lost money.

# Chapter Nine
# WHY DID PLAYERS
# WIN OR LOSE?

The preceding charts in this book illustrate that there were major differences in the financial outcomes of play for our three different types of bettors.

Further analysis of the 5,000-hand sample helps explain why the differences occurred.

## CARD COUNTER

Any good book about card counting states that the long-term financial gain by the counter occurs because he has more money on the table when his count is favorable; i.e. when his chances of winning are more favorable than the dealer's chances of winning, and when his chances of drawing a blackjack are more favorable.

The majority of the time — 80% or more — the count is either neutral or negative, and the counter will be wagering the minimum amount required to be at the table. In other words, the card counter is a minimum-bet flat bettor until the count becomes positive enough to swing the advantage in his favor by 1% or more, at which time he substantially increases his bet.

In regard to our 5,000 hands, and the Black Ace count system we used, our counter began increasing his bet when the count reached +20. Increases ranged from $60 (three times the minimum bet) to $240 (12 times the minimum bet) depending upon how positive the count became.

The key question is, "What was the card counter's win/loss rate while the count was +20 or better?"

The following chart is extrapolated from the 5,000-hand run, and lists win/loss totals for each shoe when the count was +20 or higher:

## COUNTER BETTOR
## WINNING/LOSING BETS WHEN COUNT
## REACHED PLUS 20 OR BETTER

| SHOE # | WINS | LOSSES |
|:---:|:---:|:---:|
| 1. | 1 | 3 |
| 3. | 8 | 15 |
| 5. | | 1 |
| 6. | | 1 |
| 9. | 3 | 2 |
| 12. | | 1 |
| 13. | 17 | 13 |
| 15. | 8 | 8 |
| 16. | 2 | 1 |
| 18. | 1 | |
| 19. | | 2 |
| 23. | | 5 |
| 26. | 16 | 9 |
| 27. | 1 | 9 |
| 28. | | 5 |
| 29. | 9 | 13 |
| 30. | 5 | 8 |
| 33. | 4 | 1 |
| 34. | 1 | 3 |

| SHOE # | WINS | LOSSES |
|--------|------|--------|
| 35. | 3 | 3 |
| 36. | 11 | 21 |
| 37. | 4 | 5 |
| 40. | 8 | 7 |
| 41. | 1 | 1 |
| 42. | 3 | 3 |
| 43. | 4 | 5 |
| 45. | 6 | 14 |
| 46. | 1 | 2 |
| 47. | 12 | 21 |
| 49. | 15 | 5 |
| 50. | 1 | 1 |
| 52. | 13 | 12 |
| 53. | 11 | 10 |
| 55. | 1 | 1 |
| 56. | 6 | 5 |
| 61. | 8 | 6 |
| 62. | 10 | 6 |
| 64. | 2 | 2 |
| 66. | 1 | 2 |
| 70. | 9 | 10 |
| 74. | 2 | 5 |
| 75. | 12 | 9 |
| 78. | 1 | |
| 79. | 2 | |
| 83. | 3 | 4 |
| 84. | 11 | 7 |
| 85. | 1 | |
| 87. | 5 | 6 |
| 90. | 13 | 10 |
| 91. | 10 | 11 |
| 92. | 1 | 4 |
| 94. | 3 | 5 |
| 95. | 6 | 5 |
| 96. | 8 | 8 |
| 98. | 3 | 4 |
| 99. | 3 | 1 |

| SHOE # | WINS | LOSSES |
|---|---|---|
| 100. | 2 | 6 |
| 101. | 1 | 2 |
| TOTALS: | 293 Wins | 329 Losses |
| | (42%) | (48%) |

TOTAL NUMBER OF PUSHES: 76 (10%)
Total number of shoes with at least one 20+ bet: 58
Total number of +20 (or higher) bets: 698

This chart gives the answer to the preceding question, and also explains why the card counter lost money.

The counter had 698 opportunities to raise his bet due to positive counts — about 14% of the bets made. This is in keeping with normal expectation. The problem is that he lost 48% of the bets, pushed 10% of the bets, and only won 42% of the bets. Even though he had a clear advantage over the dealer each and every time the count reached +20 or higher, actual results did not match anticipated or predicted results.

This is known in card counting lingo as "negative fluctuation," which simply means that our player lost even though he was slightly favored to win. I suspect this is why most seasoned card counters have prematurely gray hair!

An analysis of our 5,000-hand sample shows that a reversal in the outcome of less than two dozen hands would have made a major difference in the financial status of our card counter. Had the dealer received the player's cards, and the player received the dealer's cards on less than 1% of the hands dealt, the card counter's results would have changed dramatically!

# FLAT BETTOR

Our flat bettor experienced losses that are very much in line with normal expectation as predicted in most good casino gaming books. A flat bettor using perfect Basic Strategy in a six-deck game is expected to lose about one-half percent of the money wagered — and he did.

What the books don't say is that the flat bettor has a tough time recovering previous losses because of the nature of his betting style. The flat bettor in our 5,000-hand simulation experienced several losing shoes early in the game, had no strategy that allowed him to increase his initial wager during subsequent shoes, had no strategy that would have prompted him to leave the table, and continued in a negative financial state throughout the remaining shoes of play.

# PROGRESSIVE BETTOR

The progressive bettor's more successful record for the 5,000 hands of play is due to several factors.

One reason our player won more is explained by the following chart:

# RESULTS OF CONSECUTIVE WINS
# FOLLOWED BY A LOSS
# PROGRESSIVE VS. FLAT BETS

This chart compares the results of consecutive wins by a progressive bettor (who follows a $20, $30, $40, $50, $50, etc. progression) with a flat bettor (who bets $20 per hand).

| Progressive Bettor | | | Flat Bettor | | |
|---|---|---|---|---|---|
| **Win** | **Lose** | **Net Result** | **Win** | **Lose** | **Net Result** |
| 1 | 1 | $-10 | 1 | 1 | $-0- |
| 2 | 1 | +10 | 2 | 1 | +20 |
| 3 | 1 | +40 | 3 | 1 | +40 |
| 4 | 1 | +90 | 4 | 1 | +60 |
| 5 | 1 | +140 | 5 | 1 | +80 |
| 6 | 1 | +190 | 6 | 1 | +100 |
| 7 | 1 | +240 | 7 | 1 | +120 |
| 8 | 1 | +290 | 8 | 1 | +140 |
| 9 | 1 | +340 | 9 | 1 | +160 |
| 10 | 1 | +390 | 10 | 1 | +180 |

The chart illustrates why progressive systems can be more successful than flat betting when clusters of consecutive winning hands occur. Once a progressive bettor using the $20 to $50 spread wins four consecutive hands, his net profit for this cluster is 50% greater than the flat bettor's net profit, even if he loses the next hand. After seven winning hands in a row, his profits are *twice* that of the flat bettor. Even though he will eventually lose $50 — his maximum bet, compared to the flat bettor's $20 loss — his profits will still be far superior to the flat bettor's profits.

With clusters of losing hands, the progressive bettor may lose up to $30 more than the flat bettor *for one hand only*, assuming that he increased his bet due to preceding winning bets. After this one loss, where the flat bettor will lose $10 to $30 less than the progressive bettor, both players will lose equal amounts of money ($20 per hand) as long as consecutive losses continue to occur. If clusters of losing hands begin at the start of a new shoe, both players lose $20 per hand, and there is no difference in the results.

Stated differently, a progressive bettor can lose only a maximum of $30 more than a flat bettor if they both suffer 10 consecutive losing hands, but the progressive bettor can win $210 more than the flat bettor if they both enjoy 10 consecutive winning hands!

The astute reader will note that the preceding chart makes no reference to splits or double-downs. What if the progressive bettor splits or doubles his hand while at the top of his progression, and loses all bets? Obviously the $30 loss mentioned above could be several times larger.

This scenario is possible, but not probable. In fact, *just the opposite* is more likely to happen, because splits and doubles are options that generally *favor* the player. Blackjack books encourage players to take advantage of Basic Strategy advice to split or double-down, since these options improve our chances of winning more or losing less.

Another reason our progressive player had better results than the other players for the 5,000 hands of play is because our simulation closely resembled long-term win/loss expectations. Even though our players only won 45% of their bets, the clusters of winning hands — clusters that caused our progressive bettor to have more money on the table — helped make it possible for the progressive bettor to show better results for the session.

A third reason that our progressive player did better was because our players drew a higher percentage of blackjacks than would be expected in the long run. This helped both the progressive bettor and the card counter, since they both had more opportunities to have more cash on the table when blackjacks came their way.

Summarizing the data in this chapter:

1. THE CARD COUNTER LOST MORE MONEY THAN HE WON WHILE THE COUNT WAS POSITIVE, DUE TO "NEGATIVE FLUC-TUATION."

2. THE PROGRESSIVE BETTOR HAD A "TRACK RECORD" SUPERIOR TO THE COUNTER AND THE FLAT BETTOR.

Many more revealing bits of information resulted from our simulation — information that to the best of my knowledge has never been fully considered in previously published casino gaming books; information that could change your entire perspective on the game.

In the next chapter we look at the effects of consecutive wins and losses, and how important they are to our players.

# Chapter Ten
# CONSECUTIVE WINS AND LOSSES: SIMILARITIES AND CONTRASTS

One would assume that our three different types of players — the flat bettor, the progressive bettor, and the card counter — would share much in common. After all, all three used the same Basic Strategy and all three played the same cards against the same dealer's cards. They all won when the dealer busted, and they all received three to two payoffs on blackjacks. If their betting pattern was the only differentiating factor, why were their final outcomes so dissimilar?

Prior to your reading of this chapter, I have to warn you that there are lots of charts, lots of numbers, and lots of information which may be of no interest to you! Unless you're a mathematician, a statistician, or a critical analyst, you might want to turn to the last few pages of this chapter where the results of the analyses are presented. This is the most complicated and the most "technical" section in this book, and it's here because it's necessary to validate conclusions and recommendations.

Further analysis of our 5,000 hands of play indicates why one player fared better (or worse) than other players:

# AVERAGE COUNT VS.
## CONSECUTIVE WINS OR LOSSES

An assumption that I made prior to the study was that the progressive bettor's success or failure at being dealt consecutive winning or losing hands was closely associated with the composition of the deck while the clusters of wins or losses were happening.

I assumed that a series of winning hands was more likely to occur when the count was +20 or higher for the card counter, while he had an advantage over the dealer, and that the progressive bettor would *coincidentally* experience consecutive winning hands as a result of the positive count. I also assumed that a series of losing hands was much more likely to occur when the count was neutral or negative, and that both players would suffer equally.

In order to verify my beliefs, I analyzed the 5,000-hand run, and summarized the data in two charts.

The first chart is a summary of shoes that contained clusters of four or more winning bets. Also included in this chart is the *average count* that the card counter had while each of these clusters were occurring:

# SUMMARY OF
# CONSECUTIVE WINNING BETS OF FOUR OR
# MORE AND AVERAGE COUNT
# WHILE WINS WERE OCCURRING

| SHOE # | 4 OR MORE WINS | BLACK ACE AVERAGE COUNT | QUIT POINT |
|---|---|---|---|
| 1. | 4 | 7.5 | |
| 1. | 4 | 16.75 | |
| 2. | 5 | 4.20 | |
| 2. | 6 | 9.34 | |
| 2. | 5 | 7.0 | |
| 3. | 5 | 18.40 | |
| 3. | 5 | 20.8 | |
| 4. | 5 | 5.8 | |
| 4. | 6 | 2.67 | |
| 4. | 4 | 10.0 | |
| 4. | 4 | 8.5 | |
| 5. | 4 | 11.25 | |
| 6. | 4 | .75 | |
| 6. | 4 | 11.0 | |
| 7. | 5 | -1.40 | |
| 7. | 4 | 12.75 | |
| 8. | 8 | 6.75 | |
| 9. ($-165*) | 0 | N/A | ($-35**) |
| 10. | 4 | 3.5 | |
| 10. | 5 | 6.2 | |
| 10. | 4 | 12.5 | |
| 11. | 7 | 13.58 | |
| 12. | 6 | 10.34 | |
| 13. | 7 | 25.86 | |
| 14. | 4 | 9.75 | |
| 15. | 7 | 10.00 | |
| 15. | 4 | 12.25 | |
| 16. ($-120) | 0 | N/A | ($-160) |
| 17. | 5 | 11.80 | |

| SHOE # | 4 OR MORE WINS | BLACK ACE AVERAGE COUNT | QUIT POINT |
|---|---|---|---|
| 18. ($-250) | 0 | N/A | NONE |
| 19. | 10 | 9.20 | |
| 19. | 7 | 17.29 | |
| 20. | 5 | 9.40 | |
| 20. | 6 | 1.34 | |
| 20. | 5 | 2.0 | |
| 21. | 11 | 6.36 | |
| 21. | 5 | 14.40 | |
| 22. | 5 | .40 | |
| 22. | 5 | 2.60 | |
| 23. | 6 | 8.50 | |
| 24. ($-360) | 0 | N/A | ($-130) |
| 25. ($-90) | 0 | N/A | NONE |
| 26. | 4 | 7.25 | |
| 26. | 6 | 19.17 | |
| 26. | 5 | 21.20 | |
| 27. | 4 | 12.0 | |
| 27. | 5 | 12.0 | |
| 28. | 4 | -4.0 | |
| 28. | 8 | 10.88 | |
| 29. | 4 | 17.75 | |
| 29. | 4 | 17.75 | |
| 30. | 4 | 8.50 | |
| 31. | 8 | 9.86 | |
| 31. | 4 | 9.00 | |
| 32. | 7 | 9.29 | |
| 33. | 5 | 13.20 | |
| 33. | 5 | 20.60 | |
| 34. ($-370) | 0 | N/A | ($-315) |
| 35. | 6 | 7.0 | |
| 36. (-430) | 0 | N/A | ($-230) |
| 37. | 6 | 5.67 | |
| 37. | 5 | 19.0 | |
| 38. | 7 | 6.58 | |
| 38. | 4 | 5.25 | |

| SHOE # | 4 OR MORE WINS | BLACK ACE AVERAGE COUNT | QUIT POINT |
|---|---|---|---|
| 38. | 4 | 7.0 | |
| 38. | 4 | 10.75 | |
| 39. | 4 | 7.25 | |
| 39. | 6 | 10.34 | |
| 39. | 4 | 12.75 | |
| 39. | 4 | 14.75 | |
| 40. | 5 | 8.0 | |
| 40. | 5 | 9.0 | |
| 40. | 5 | 21.0 | |
| 40. | 5 | 19.0 | |
| 41. | 6 | 15.50 | |
| 41. | 7 | 11.86 | |
| 42. | 4 | 13.50 | |
| 43. | 6 | 10.34 | |
| 44. | 4 | 11.50 | |
| 44. | 5 | 9.0 | |
| 44. | 7 | 15.29 | |
| 45. | 7 | 2.29 | |
| 46. | 4 | 6.75 | |
| 46. | 6 | 15.17 | |
| 46. | 7 | 17.29 | |
| 47. | 5 | 20.0 | |
| 47. | 5 | 20.8 | |
| 48. | 4 | 9.50 | |
| 48. | 7 | 8.15 | |
| 49. | 5 | 18.80 | |
| 49. | 4 | 21.00 | |
| 49. | 5 | 20.8 | |
| 50. | 7 | 13.0 | |
| 51. | 5 | 3.40 | |
| 52. | 5 | 12.0 | |
| 52. | 5 | 22.0 | |
| 53. | 5 | 18.0 | |
| 53. | 7 | 20.43 | |
| 54. | 5 | 6.8 | |

| SHOE # | 4 OR MORE WINS | BLACK ACE AVERAGE COUNT | QUIT POINT |
|---|---|---|---|
| 54. | 10 | 11.4 | |
| 55. | 5 | 8.0 | |
| 56. | 6 | 6.50 | |
| 56. | 4 | 22.5 | |
| 57. | 4 | 8.75 | |
| 57. | 5 | 11.0 | |
| 58. | 6 | 4.84 | |
| 58. | 4 | 4.0 | |
| 59. | 4 | 16.0 | |
| 60. | 4 | 16.0 | |
| 61. | 10 | 9.90 | |
| 62. | 6 | 8.84 | |
| 62. | 4 | 19.75 | |
| 63. | 5 | 5.80 | |
| 64. ($-440) | 0 | N/A | ($-130) |
| 65. ($-275) | 0 | N/A | NONE |
| 66. | 4 | 13.5 | |
| 67. | 4 | 10.75 | |
| 67. | 5 | 9.40 | |
| 68. | 5 | 16.6 | |
| 69. | 5 | -2.0 | |
| 70. | 4 | 19.75 | |
| 71. | 5 | 7.0 | |
| 71. | 4 | 11.25 | |
| 72. | 4 | 7.75 | |
| 73. | 9 | 5.23 | |
| 73. | 4 | 10.0 | |
| 74. | 5 | 15.4 | |
| 74. | 4 | 13.0 | |
| 74. | 6 | 18.0 | |
| 75. | 7 | 16.0 | |
| 75. | 5 | 21.8 | |
| 76. | 5 | 10.6 | |
| 76. | 5 | 15.6 | |
| 76. | 6 | 14.17 | |

| SHOE # | 4 OR MORE WINS | BLACK ACE AVERAGE COUNT | QUIT POINT |
|---|---|---|---|
| 77. | 4 | 2.25 | |
| 77. | 5 | -1.75 | |
| 77. | 4 | 7.50 | |
| 78. | 4 | 11.25 | |
| 78. | 4 | 12.5 | |
| 78. | 4 | 14.75 | |
| 79. | 6 | 17.34 | |
| 79. | 4 | 7.5 | |
| 80. | 4 | 15.0 | |
| 80. | 4 | 13.5 | |
| 81. | 5 | 6.40 | |
| 81. | 10 | 13.5 | |
| 82. | 4 | 14.25 | |
| 82. | 5 | 5.60 | |
| 83. | 10 | 9.60 | |
| 84. | 8 | 6.25 | |
| 84. | 5 | 23.0 | |
| 85. | 4 | 5.75 | |
| 85. | 4 | 14.25 | |
| 85. | 5 | 14.0 | |
| 85. | 6 | 17.5 | |
| 86. | 9 | 11.34 | |
| 86. | 4 | 16.0 | |
| 87. ($-275) | 0 | N/A | ($-70) |
| 88. | 5 | 10.8 | |
| 88. | 4 | 8.25 | |
| 89. | 4 | 2.0 | |
| 90. ($0) | 0 | N/A | ($-150) |
| 91. | 9 | 16.0 | |
| 92. | 5 | 8.0 | |
| 93. | 5 | 12.0 | |
| 93. | 4 | 11.75 | |
| 93. | 6 | 15.50 | |
| 94. | 0 | N/A | ($-10) |
| 95. ($-100) | 0 | N/A | ($-250) |

| SHOE # | 4 OR MORE WINS | BLACK ACE AVERAGE COUNT | QUIT POINT |
|---|---|---|---|
| 96. ($-50) | 0 | N/A | ($-350) |
| 97. | 4 | 7.0 | |
| 97. | 4 | 3.83 | |
| 98. | 0 | N/A | ($-120) |
| 99. | 7 | 12.0 | |
| 99. | 4 | 18.0 | |
| 99. | 5 | 20.0 | |
| 100. | 4 | 17.0 | |
| 101. | 4 | 15.0 | |
| 102. | 4 | 13.0 | |
| 102. | 4 | 10.0 | |
| 102. | 5 | 19.0 | |
| TOTALS: | 166 | 1,892.20 | |

\* End of shoe result for progressive bettor.
\*\* Quit point for progressive bettor.

## Summary of Data

1. Fifteen shoes had no four consecutive bet winning "runs." The progressive bettor lost $3,490 on the 15 shoes with no strings of four or more winning bets, for an average loss of $233 per shoe. The progressive bettor lost on every one of these 15 shoes.

2. The 15 losing shoes had quit points which totaled $-1,220. The player lost $2,435 more by continuing to play until the end of the shoes.

3. A breakdown of the number of winning bets in each string is as follows:

| | |
|---|---|
| Four consecutive winning bets: | 66 |
| Five consecutive winning bets: | 53 |
| Six consecutive winning bets: | 20 |
| Seven consecutive winning bets: | 15 |
| Eight consecutive winning bets: | 4 |
| Nine consecutive winning bets: | 3 |
| Ten consecutive winning bets: | 5 |
| Eleven or more consecutive: | 1 |
| Total: | 167 |

4. The average count for all strings of consecutive winning bets of four or more was (1,892.20 divided by 167): 11.33. The average count for all strings of six or more consecutive winning bets was (550.41 divided by 48): 11.47. The average count for the five strings of 10 consecutive winning bets was (53.60 divided by 5): 10.72.

5. The total number of individual winning bets that occurred in strings of four or more consecutive wins was 874. The total number of wins that occurred in the 102 shoes was 2,534. Consequently, the progressive bettor was winning from $30 (four consecutive wins) to $260 (11 consecutive wins) *more* than the flat bettor for 29% of the time they were winning (874 divided by 2,534).

Observation: My initial assumption was that there would be a direct relationship between the success of the progressive player and the success of the card counter. I assumed that the progressive bettor would share the benefits of a very positive count and be much more likely to experience many consecutive winning bets when the count was very positive.

This doesn't appear to be the case! There were only 13 occasions when the progressive player experienced a run of four or more consecutive wins when the count was 20 or higher, out of a total of 167 occasions when the progressive bettor experienced four or more consecutive winning bets! Even though the count was slightly positive for runs of four or more consecutive wins, there appears to be no direct relationship between these two different styles of playing the game.

An explanation of the columns in the preceding chart is as follows:

1. Shoe #: Lists a shoe in which a cluster of four or more consecutive wins occurred. The shoe number is repeated if more than one cluster occurred in the shoe.

2. Four or More Wins: The number of consecutive wins that occurred prior to a loss in each shoe.

3. Black Ace Average Count: The average count during each cluster of four or more wins.

4. Quit Point: This column relates to a later chapter in the book, and will be discussed when this element of progressive betting is presented.

An explanation of how to read the chart: In Shoe #1, there were two separate runs of four consecutive winning hands. The Black Ace count average for the first run of winning bets was 7.5, derived by adding up the running count for each hand, and dividing by the number of consecutive winning hands. An additional run of four consecutive winning hands occurred later in the same shoe, and the average count while these bets were being won was 16.75.

Question: "Is the card counter experiencing a high positive count while clusters of winning bets are happening?" The answer appears to be, "NO!"

There were 167 clusters of consecutive wins

of four or more bets, and the average count was 11.33 while these clusters were occurring. Since our card counter started each shoe with a count of +8, and didn't increase his bet until the count reached +20, a count of 11.33, although slightly positive, doesn't indicate that four or more consecutive wins occurred because of a high count.

Even when we look at the average count for six or more consecutive wins (11.74), or the average count for the five clusters of 10 consecutive wins (10.72), there is *no evidence* to indicate that the count will be highly positive while clusters of consecutive winning hands are occurring.

In fact, there were only 13 occasions when the progressive player enjoyed a run of four or more consecutive wins while the count was +20 or higher, out of a total of 167 occasions when four or more consecutive wins occurred.

So, what does this data indicate? It indicates that there is *no obvious relationship between a positive count and consecutive winning wagers.*

Another question we might ask is, "How did the flat bettor do while the progressive bettor was winning four or more consecutive hands?" The answer to this question is provocative, to say the least!

The total number of individual winning bets that occurred in clusters of four or more was 874, out of a total of 2,534 winning bets. Consequently, the progressive bettor was winning $30 (four consecutive wins) to $260 (11 consecutive wins) *more per cluster* than the flat bettor for 29% of the time they were playing the 102 shoes (874 divided by 2,534)!

But what about consecutive *losing* bets of

four or more? Was the count negative, and did it adversely affect the three players?

The following chart — the opposite of the previous chart — reveals answers to these questions.

## SUMMARY OF CONSECUTIVE LOSING BETS OF FOUR OR MORE AND AVERAGE COUNT WHILE LOSSES WERE OCCURRING

| SHOE # | FOUR OR MORE LOSSES | BLACK ACE AVERAGE COUNT |
|--------|---------------------|-------------------------|
| 1. | 4 | 0.0 |
| 1. | 5 | 13.6 |
| 2. | 6 | 10.0 |
| 3. | 5 | 23.0 |
| 4. | 4 | 4.0 |
| 5. | 6 | 2.67 |
| 5. | 4 | -2.50 |
| 6. | 5 | 2.0 |
| 6. | 5 | 8.40 |
| 7. | 4 | 5.25 |
| 7. | 4 | -6.25 |
| 7. | 4 | 4.75 |
| 8. | 4 | 6.25 |
| 9. | 5 | 18.20 |
| 9. | 4 | 12.75 |
| 9. | 4 | 16.0 |
| 10. | 5 | 8.60 |
| 11. | 4 | 6.25 |
| 12. | 4 | 17.0 |
| 13. | 6 | 18.0 |
| 13. | 5 | 17.60 |
| 14. | 4 | 16.75 |
| 14. | 4 | 9.75 |
| 15. | 4 | 13.25 |

| SHOE # | FOUR OR MORE LOSSES | BLACK ACE AVERAGE COUNT |
|---|---|---|
| 16. | 4 | 16.25 |
| 17. | 5 | 11.80 |
| 17. | 4 | 14.75 |
| 19. | 6 | 8.34 |
| 19. | 4 | 11.0 |
| 19. | 5 | 17.60 |
| 19. | 4 | 18.75 |
| 19. | 4 | 16.75 |
| 20. | 8 | 6.63 |
| 21. | 6 | 11.0 |
| 21. | 4 | 16.0 |
| 23. | 5 | 8.80 |
| 23. | 4 | 13.75 |
| 23. | 7 | 12.15 |
| 23. | 4 | 16.25 |
| 23. | 4 | 20.0 |
| 24. | 4 | 2.50 |
| 24. | 5 | 11.20 |
| 24. | 5 | 13.40 |
| 27. | 5 | 8.40 |
| 27. | 5 | 18.60 |
| 27. | 4 | 20.0 |
| 28. | 7 | 20.72 |
| 29. | 4 | 6.75 |
| 29. | 4 | 21.25 |
| 30. | 4 | 18.25 |
| 30. | 4 | 18.25 |
| 30. | 5 | 11.60 |
| 31. | 6 | 9.50 |
| 32. | 4 | 9.50 |
| 33. | 6 | 9.84 |
| 34. | 4 | 12.5 |
| 36. | 6 | 27.0 |
| 36. | 7 | 23.15 |
| 37. | 6 | 10.34 |

| SHOE # | FOUR OR MORE LOSSES | BLACK ACE AVERAGE COUNT |
|---|---|---|
| 38. | 4 | 13.5 |
| 39. | 5 | 7.0 |
| 39. | 4 | 11.0 |
| 40. | 4 | 20.25 |
| 42. | 5 | 10.60 |
| 42. | 4 | 6.0 |
| 42. | 4 | 19.0 |
| 43. | 5 | 12.6 |
| 43. | 8 | 4.88 |
| 44. | 5 | 14.20 |
| 44. | 5 | 16.0 |
| 44. | 4 | 14.0 |
| 45. | 4 | 5.75 |
| 45. | 5 | 8.20 |
| 45. | 6 | 23.0 |
| 46. | 4 | 13.50 |
| 47. | 5 | 13.0 |
| 47. | 6 | 20.67 |
| 47. | 4 | 25.25 |
| 46. | 6 | 21.34 |
| 48. | 5 | 7.40 |
| 50. | 4 | 18.75 |
| 50. | 4 | 14.25 |
| 50. | 4 | 13.0 |
| 51. | 4 | 15.0 |
| 52. | 6 | 22.84 |
| 54. | 10 | 2.30 |
| 54. | 4 | -.75 |
| 54. | 4 | 4.0 |
| 55. | 4 | 14.0 |
| 56. | 4 | 23.50 |
| 58. | 4 | 14.5 |
| 59. | 8 | 12.25 |
| 59. | 4 | 16.0 |
| 59. | 5 | 14.20 |

| SHOE # | FOUR OR MORE LOSSES | BLACK ACE AVERAGE COUNT |
|---|---|---|
| 60. | 4 | 8.50 |
| 61. | 4 | 18.0 |
| 62. | 4 | 15.25 |
| 63. | 5 | 9.60 |
| 63. | 4 | 11.0 |
| 63. | 4 | 15.25 |
| 64. | 6 | 10.50 |
| 64. | 4 | 18.25 |
| 64. | 4 | 16.5 |
| 65. | 5 | 4.20 |
| 65. | 4 | 1.25 |
| 66. | 4 | 11.0 |
| 67. | 5 | 12.40 |
| 67. | 4 | 8.75 |
| 68. | 4 | 4.0 |
| 68. | 5 | 12.20 |
| 69. | 6 | 9.50 |
| 69. | 4 | -1.50 |
| 70. | 7 | 11.72 |
| 71. | 6 | 12.84 |
| 72. | 4 | 12.50 |
| 72. | 4 | 17.25 |
| 73. | 6 | 6.84 |
| 73. | 7 | 6.43 |
| 73. | 4 | 5.75 |
| 75. | 5 | 9.60 |
| 77. | 5 | 5.80 |
| 78. | 4 | 17.0 |
| 79. | 9 | 11.78 |
| 79. | 4 | 9.50 |
| 79. | 4 | 9.75 |
| 80. | 4 | 6.50 |
| 80. | 4 | 12.75 |
| 80. | 4 | 11.0 |
| 82. | 4 | 10.25 |

| SHOE # | FOUR OR MORE LOSSES | BLACK ACE AVERAGE COUNT |
|---|---|---|
| 82. | 4 | 10.75 |
| 83. | 4 | 13.0 |
| 83. | 9 | 15.78 |
| 83. | 4 | 18.25 |
| 84. | 4 | 16.25 |
| 84. | 5 | 18.40 |
| 85. | 4 | 10.75 |
| 86. | 4 | 10.50 |
| 86. | 4 | 15.25 |
| 87. | 8 | 7.50 |
| 87. | 4 | 17.0 |
| 88. | 4 | 13.0 |
| 89. | 5 | 1.20 |
| 90. | 5 | 17.40 |
| 90. | 6 | 17.0 |
| 93. | 10 | 11.80 |
| 95. | 4 | 1.0 |
| 95. | 6 | 7.84 |
| 95. | 4 | 16.75 |
| 96. | 5 | 10.40 |
| 96. | 4 | 8.25 |
| 97. | 4 | 11.25 |
| 97. | 6 | 6.50 |
| 97. | 5 | 8.20 |
| 100. | 6 | 12.50 |
| 101. | 4 | 8.0 |
| 101. | 4 | 16.25 |
| 102. | 5 | 11.60 |
| 102. | 5 | 16.0 |
| 102. | 5 | 18.80 |
| 160 RUNS | 775 BETS TOTAL COUNT (FOUR OR MORE LOSSES) | 1,933.45 (BLACK ACE AVERAGE COUNT) |

Average count for runs of four or more consecutive losses: 12.09

Total # of shoes with at least one run of four or more consecutive losses: 86

Total # of runs of four or more consecutive losses: 160

Total # of shoes with no consecutive losses of four or more hands: 16

## SUMMARY OF SHOES WITH NO CONSECUTIVE LOSSES OF FOUR OR MORE HANDS

| SHOE# | NET $ FOR PROGRESSIVE BETTOR |
|-------|------------------------------|
| 18. | $-250 |
| 22. | 175 |
| 25. | -90 |
| 26. | 320 |
| 35. | 170 |
| 41. | 270 |
| 49. | 430 |
| 53. | 290 |
| 57. | 75 |
| 74. | 80 |
| 76. | 250 |
| 91. | 405 |
| 92. | -40 |
| 94. | -10 |
| 98. | -120 |
| 99. | 475 |
| 16 Shoes | $2,430 |

## FREQUENCY SUMMARY

| | |
|---|---|
| Four consecutive losing bets: | 87 |
| Five consecutive losing bets: | 38 |
| Six consecutive losing bets: | 22 |
| Seven consecutive losing bets: | 5 |
| Eight consecutive losing bets: | 4 |

| | |
|---|---|
| Nine consecutive losing bets: | 2 |
| Ten consecutive losing bets: | 2 |
| Eleven or more consecutive losing bets: | 0 |
| | Total: 160 |

Total # of runs of five or more consecutive losing bets: 73 (46% of losing runs of four or more).

The preceding chart shows that there were 160 occasions when our players suffered through clusters of four or more consecutive losses, and that 775 bets were lost while these clusters were occurring. This compares to 167 occasions when our players were enjoying clusters of four or more wins while placing 874 bets.

This chart supports the philosophy of the progressive better, in that clusters of winning and losing bets tend to happen with about the same frequency. More on this later . . .

What about the average count while clusters of four or more consecutive losses are occurring?

Analysis of the bets shows that the average count during these losing periods was 12.09, *slightly more positive* than the average count while our players were winning four or more consecutive bets. Once again there appears to be no direct relationship between consecutive wins or losses and the average count while these wins or losses were happening.

This conclusion leads me to doubt the potential effectiveness of a common tactic employed by card counting teams. The tactic works like this: A card counter plays at a table and makes small wagers while waiting for an increase in the count. When the count becomes very positive, he secretly signals a partner who joins the game and makes large bets while the count is very positive. Hypothetically the partner will win large sums of money, and the casino will not realize that a card counting team is present. Since our study doesn't substantiate the fact that consecutive wins occur more frequently during periods of high positive counts, I doubt the overall effectiveness of this team tactic.

In all fairness to card counters, several have told me that this method of team play doesn't require that the "high-roller" partner win consecutive bets. He's only expected to win more hands than he loses while the count is positive, and will enjoy a net profit by placing large wagers while the count favors him.

What about the relationship between our flat bettor and our progressive bettor while consecutive losses were occurring? In this case our flat bettor *lost less* than the progressive bettor, since the progressive bettor often loses a bet after winning a bet, and will have $10 to $30 more on the table due to his previous progression. The maximum difference in total losses will be $30, regardless of the length of the losing cluster because each bettor equally loses $20 per bet as long as the losing cluster continues.

A final "head-to-head" comparison of winning and losing "runs," or clusters, will further clarify the effects of this aspect of the game.

# COMPARISON OF
# WINNING AND LOSING "RUNS"

|  | WINNING | LOSING |
|---|---|---|
| 1. Number of shoes with at least one series of four or more consecutive wins or losses: | 166 | 160 |
| 2. Number of shoes with no consecutive series of wins or losses of four or more bets: | 15 | 16 |
| 3. Average count while runs were occurring: | 11.33 | 12.09 |
| 4. Total number of net winning or losing bets that occurred as part of runs: | 874 | 775 |
| 5. Frequency of runs of winning or losing bets: |  |  |
| Four consecutive bets | 66 | 87 |
| Five consecutive bets | 52 | 38 |
| Six consecutive bets | 20 | 22 |
| Seven consecutive bets | 15 | 5 |
| Eight consecutive bets | 4 | 4 |
| Nine consecutive bets | 3 | 2 |
| Ten consecutive bets | 5 | 2 |
| Eleven or more consecutive bets | 1 | 0 |
| Totals: | 167 | 160 |

6. Shoes with no consecutive runs of four or more net wins or losses, and the effect on the progressive bettor:

Fifteen shoes had no consecutive runs of four or more winning bets, which resulted in $3,490 in losses (an average of $-233 per shoe) for the progressive bettor. Our progressive bettor lost money on all of these shoes.

Sixteen shoes had no consecutive runs of four or more losing bets, which resulted in profits of $2,430 (an average of $+152 per shoe) for the progressive bettor. Our progressive bettor profited on 11 of 16 shoes.

The preceding illustration shows that shoes with winning and losing clusters tend to occur with about the same frequency, and that shoes with no winning or losing clusters also occur with about the same frequency.

This illustration also shows that the average count is not a predictor of winning or losing clusters since the count is almost identical for both events.

The fourth item in the illustration is significant. All of our players won 99 more bets while winning clusters were occurring than they lost while losing clusters were occurring, even though the number of winning and losing clusters were almost identical.

I attribute much of this imbalance to the fact that players are allowed to split or double-down when the odds of winning are in their favor. By taking advantage of player-friendly rules, all of our players were able to place more bets when they were more likely to win.

Consecutive losses, however, were more likely to occur when our players drew hands which couldn't be split or doubled, or when they drew "stiffs" and busted prior to the dealer's draw. In either case, single bets were the only option.

The third possible reason for the difference between numbers of wins and losses might be —

you guessed it — Lady Luck! Although most experts discount the possibility that good fortune can affect long-term play, it's possible that a number of short-term events may have occurred sequentially, and helped all of our players to enjoy more winning bets while clusters were happening.

As Item #5 shows, our players had many more winning clusters of five and seven consecutive wins than they had losing clusters of five and seven consecutive losses. All players benefited from these disparities, but the progressive player benefited more often because of his betting progression.

Since our flat bettor was betting the same $20 on every initial bet, and our card counter was essentially a flat bettor about 85% of the time due to neutral or negative counts, neither of them was capable of drawing maximum financial benefit from these winning clusters.

The final portion of our study of winning and losing clusters has to do with the "extremes." How were our players affected by shoes that had *no* clusters of winning or losing bets?

Item #6 shows that our progressive bettor was seriously affected by these unlikely shoes — unlikely because only 31 of 102 shoes (about 30%) were played without at least one series of four or more consecutive winning or losing bets.

Our progressive bettor had end-of-shoe losses of $3,490 on the 15 shoes with no consecutive runs of four or more winning bets because he never advanced far enough into his progression to profit from this betting system. In fact, he lost money on *every shoe* that didn't have at least one run of four or more consecutive winning bets.

On the other hand, he won money on 11 of

16 shoes when there were no runs of four or more consecutive losing bets, for a net profit of $2,430. Obviously the lack of clusters of losing bets meant that there was a probability of a higher number of consecutive winning clusters, which led to our progressive player's profits.

Based on the preceding information, you can see that shoes that contain several sequences of consecutive winning bets will be very beneficial, whereas shoes that contain several clusters of consecutive losing bets will be harmful to a progressive bettor.

The data analyzed in this chapter suggests the following:

1. There appears to be no direct relationship between consecutive winning or losing bets and the card counter's "count" while these consecutive wins or losses are occurring.

2. The progressive bettor is a guaranteed loser if shoes don't contain at least *one cluster* of winning bets.

3. By not honoring "quit points" (explained in the next chapter) the progressive bettor lost *twice as much* as he would have lost had he quit play after suffering losses on four consecutive hands.

4. Due to positive progression, the progressive bettor won *more* than the flat bettor on 29% of all bets made during the 5,000 hands of play.

5. The progressive bettor is much more likely to have a winning shoe if no clusters of four or more losing bets occur.

6. Winning and losing clusters tend to occur with about the same frequency, and shoes with a *total absence* of winning and losing clusters also occur with about the same frequency.

The obvious question is, "How can I avoid

playing shoes which have clusters of losing bets?" The next chapter of this book answers this question. In earlier chapters I made reference to something called "quit points." Quit points are my method of avoiding losing shoes, and, as improbable as it may seem, they work!

# Chapter Eleven
# PROGRESSIVE QUIT POINTS

There's another element to my progressive betting strategy that is unique, and so radical and so revolutionary that I've held off describing it until this point in the book. Had I presented this twist in strategy in an earlier chapter, you might have decided that I was a blithering idiot and thrown this book in the trash can! Or worse yet, returned it to me or the publisher for a refund!

Hopefully, you now see some value in Positive Progressive Betting, and can make a "leap in faith" and accept the credibility of the contents of this chapter.

Before I explain Progressive Quit Points and how they can substantially improve your financial success at blackjack, here is a bit of philosophical background. Many years ago I read a short story about a trainer who was working with an amateur boxer. The young boxer had just been knocked out by his opponent, and the trainer was chastising him while he was reviving him. "What's the matter with you?" he asked. "That man was beating the hell out of you, and you *leaned into his punches!* No wonder you're flat on the mat. There's a time to fight, and there's a time to back off. You should have backed off!" I don't remember the name of the author of this story, but his message came through with great clarity and I've lived the better part of a very good life by heeding his words, "Don't lean into a punch!"

Several years ago it occurred to me that "backing off" when you're getting your brains beat out could apply to blackjack in the same way that it applied to other aspects of my life. The Progressive Quit Point is my way of inculcating the "back off" philosophy into the game of blackjack, and was developed through a process of trial and error.

Let me forewarn you that the strategy move I'm about to explain, to the best of my knowledge, *has never been mentioned or advocated in any other casino gaming book.* Most gaming experts recommend money management techniques which suggest that the player always leave the casino with profits — "take the money and run," as Henry Tamburin would say. Some authors encourage players to always put aside a portion of their winnings, and as Frank Scoblete would say, "Never, never take it back out of your pocket!" But the strategy that I recommend as an improvement in positive progressive betting has never been presented.

Frankly, prior to the completion of our 5,000-hand analysis I had no definitive evidence of how truly beneficial this strategy could be. I've been using a Progressive Quit Point for about two years, and my number of winning sessions and the amount that I win has *dramatically increased.*

In our 5,000-hand simulation, the progressive bettor would have won $1,890 by using the Progressive Quit Point — a net increase of $1,920! The use of a quit point caused our progressive bettor to be a substantial winner rather than a small loser!

Now that I have your attention, I'll answer the question, "What's a quit point?"

For most of my blackjack career I never considered leaving a table just because I was losing, even when I was losing many hands in a row. I always assumed that the tide would turn and that I'd win back my losses when I got "hot." In other words, I was "leaning into a punch" — aggressively competing with a dealer who was hammering me.

Eventually it occurred to me that "backing off" might be the wiser and more financially rewarding path to take. I realized that beating a dealer on a hot streak is *not* the object of the game; *winning money* is the object of the game!

A Quit Point is a preplanned commitment to *stop play* — leave the table — anytime during a shoe after losing a predetermined number of consecutive bets. My personal strategy is to quit play after suffering net losses on four consecutive hands, whether it be at the start, in the middle of, or near the end of a shoe, and regardless of my current running total for the shoe. If I'm up $100 for the shoe after net losses on four consecutive hands, I quit; if I'm down $100, I still quit.

This same strategy — quit play after net losses on four consecutive hands — was applied to our 5,000-hand simulation, and resulted in a major increase in the progressive player's profits. The $1,890 that he won was a *direct result* of this quit-play strategy.

The following chart illustrates the shoe-by-shoe results when the quit point was honored:

## PROGRESSIVE BETTOR
## $20-$30-$40-$50 PROGRESSION RESULTS OF PLAY WITH "QUIT POINT" HONORED

The following list illustrates the result of 5,000 hands of play (102 shoes) wherein the player discontinued playing a shoe if four consecutive hands were lost.

The amount won or lost is recorded as the total for that shoe, and the player resumed play at the start of a new shoe. If no "quit point" occurred (the loss of four consecutive hands) the result for each completed shoe is recorded. The player always began a new shoe at the $20 bet level.

| SHOE # | RESULT | RUNNING TOTAL |
|:---:|:---:|:---:|
| 1. | $ +40 | $ +40 |
| 2. | +215 | +255 |
| 3. | +45 | +300 |
| 4. | +90 | +390 |
| 5. | −60 | +330 |
| 6. | −50 | +280 |
| 7. | −30 | +250 |
| 8. | −90 | +160 |
| 9. | −35 | +125 |
| 10. | +230 | +355 |
| 11. | −125 | +230 |
| 12. | −80 | +150 |
| 13. | −100 | +50 |
| 14. | −60 | −10 |
| 15. | +140 | +130 |
| 16. | −160 | −30 |
| 17. | −150 | −180 |
| 18. | −250 | −430 |
| 19. | −80 | −510 |
| 20. | +380 | −130 |
| 21. | +360 | +230 |
| 22. | +175 | +405 |
| 23. | −80 | +325 |
| 24. | −130 | +195 |
| 25. | −90 | +105 |
| 26. | +320 | +425 |
| 27. | −70 | +355 |
| 28. | +155 | +510 |
| 29. | −30 | +480 |
| 30. | −90 | +390 |

| SHOE # | RESULT | RUNNING TOTAL |
|--------|--------|---------------|
| 31. | +265 | +655 |
| 32. | −30 | +625 |
| 33. | −130 | +495 |
| 34. | −315 | +180 |
| 35. | +170 | +350 |
| 36. | −230 | +120 |
| 37. | −175 | −55 |
| 38. | +95 | +40 |
| 39. | −110 | −70 |
| 40. | +285 | +215 |
| 41. | +270 | +485 |
| 42. | −125 | +360 |
| 43. | +110 | +470 |
| 44. | +30 | +500 |
| 45. | −60 | +440 |
| 46. | −20 | +420 |
| 47. | −90 | +330 |
| 48. | −60 | +270 |
| 49. | +430 | +700 |
| 50. | −15 | +685 |
| 51. | −160 | +525 |
| 52. | +30 | +555 |
| 53. | +290 | +845 |
| 54. | +40 | +885 |
| 55. | +70 | +955 |
| 56. | +240 | +1,195 |
| 57. | +75 | +1,270 |
| 58. | +30 | +1,300 |
| 59. | −60 | +1,240 |
| 60. | −70 | +1,170 |
| 61. | +135 | +1,305 |
| 62. | −55 | +1,250 |
| 63. | −10 | +1,240 |
| 64. | −130 | +1,110 |
| 65. | −100 | +1,010 |
| 66. | −60 | +950 |
| 67. | −45 | +905 |

| SHOE # | RESULT | RUNNING TOTAL |
|--------|--------|---------------|
| 68. | −110 | +795 |
| 69. | −150 | +645 |
| 70. | −150 | +495 |
| 71. | −230 | +265 |
| 72. | −100 | +165 |
| 73. | +85 | +250 |
| 74. | +80 | +330 |
| 75. | −50 | +280 |
| 76. | +250 | +530 |
| 77. | +195 | +725 |
| 78. | +185 | +910 |
| 79. | −200 | +710 |
| 80. | −110 | +600 |
| 81. | +290 | +890 |
| 82. | −90 | +800 |
| 83. | +310 | +1,110 |
| 84. | +160 | +1,270 |
| 85. | +40 | +1,310 |
| 86. | −50 | +1,260 |
| 87. | −70 | +1,190 |
| 88. | +155 | +1,345 |
| 89. | −165 | +1,180 |
| 90. | −0− | +1,180 |
| 91. | +405 | +1,585 |
| 92. | −0− | +1,585 |
| 93. | +190 | +1,775 |
| 94. | −10 | +1,765 |
| 95. | −100 | +1,665 |
| 96. | −50 | +1,615 |
| 97. | −50 | +1,565 |
| 98. | −120 | +1,445 |
| 99. | +475 | +1,920 |
| 100. | −80 | +1,840 |
| 101. | −130 | +1,710 |
| 102. | +180 | +1,890 |
| Total: | $+1,890 | |

Note: Had the player played every shoe to completion, his net loss would have been $30. By playing the "quit point" method, his profits would have totaled $1,890 — an increase of $1,920 in net profit!

The dollar amount listed for each shoe is either the running total at the end of the shoe, or the running total during the shoe after losses on four consecutive hands. On 88 occasions, our progressive bettor would have quit play during a shoe rather than at the end of a shoe, and would have waited for the start of a new shoe or moved to a new table and waited for the start of a new shoe. Obviously, he played fewer hands than the progressive bettor who remained at the table through the conclusion of every shoe, and yet his profits were much greater! Interesting, very interesting! Our progressive player using a quit point wasn't "leaning into a punch" — he backed off — and enjoyed much better profits as a result.

In an earlier chapter we discussed the idea that players like the option of being ahead of the casino if they choose to end a session of play. We illustrated that the Positive Progressive bettor had the best track record in this regard, and was ahead of the casino at the end of 26 of 102 shoes — about 27% of the time. By applying the Quit Point tactic, the Positive Progressive better greatly improved his position, and was ahead of the casino at the end of 94 out of 102 shoes — about 93% of the time!

The Quit Point strategy was obviously profitable for the Positive Progressive bettor. And the question arises: "What about our other two players? Would they have gained anything by using the same Quit Point strategy?"

To answer this question, I recorded what happened when the flat bettor and the card counter

quit play after losses on four consecutive hands —
the same strategy used by the progressive bettor.
The following chart illustrates the financial results:

## END-OF-SHOE RESULTS
## 102 SHOES WITH QUIT POINT APPLIED
## FLAT BETTOR AND CARD COUNTER

| SHOE # | FLAT BETTOR | RUNNING TOTAL | CARD COUNTER | RUNNING TOTAL |
|---|---|---|---|---|
| 1. | $+80 | $+80 | $+80 | $+80 |
| 2. | +90 | +170 | +90 | +170 |
| 3. | +10 | +180 | −220 | −50 |
| 4. | +90 | +270 | +90 | +40 |
| 5. | +220 | +220 | −50 | −10 |
| 6. | −30 | +190 | −30 | −40 |
| 7. | −30 | +160 | −30 | −70 |
| 8. | −80 | +80 | −80 | −150 |
| 9. | −10 | +70 | −10 | −160 |
| 10. | +200 | +270 | +200 | +40 |
| 11. | −80 | +190 | −80 | −40 |
| 12. | −60 | +130 | −60 | −100 |
| 13. | −100 | +30 | −180 | −280 |
| 14. | −100 | −70 | −100 | −380 |
| 15. | +80 | +10 | +80 | −300 |
| 16. | −80 | −70 | 0 | −300 |
| 17. | −140 | −210 | −140 | −440 |
| 18. | −90 | −300 | −50 | −490 |
| 19. | −80 | −380 | −80 | −570 |
| 20. | +190 | −190 | +190 | −380 |
| 21. | +130 | −60 | +130 | −250 |
| 22. | +160 | +100 | +160 | −90 |
| 23. | −80 | +20 | −80 | −170 |
| 24. | −100 | −80 | −100 | −270 |
| 25. | +10 | −70 | +10 | −260 |
| 26. | +190 | +120 | +290 | +30 |
| 27. | −60 | +60 | −60 | −30 |

| SHOE # | FLAT BETTOR | RUNNING TOTAL | CARD COUNTER | RUNNING TOTAL |
|---|---|---|---|---|
| 28. | +110 | +170 | +70 | +40 |
| 29. | −20 | +150 | −20 | +20 |
| 30. | −40 | +110 | −120 | −100 |
| 31. | +140 | +250 | +140 | +40 |
| 32. | −30 | +220 | −30 | +10 |
| 33. | +20 | +240 | +280 | +290 |
| 34. | −180 | +60 | −180 | +110 |
| 35. | +170 | +230 | +130 | +240 |
| 36. | −160 | +70 | −720 | −480 |
| 37. | −60 | +10 | −60 | −540 |
| 38. | +130 | +140 | +130 | −410 |
| 39. | −50 | +90 | −50 | −460 |
| 40. | +130 | +220 | +190 | −270 |
| 41. | +250 | +470 | +330 | +60 |
| 42. | −20 | +450 | −20 | +40 |
| 43. | +40 | +490 | +40 | +80 |
| 44. | +10 | +500 | +10 | +90 |
| 45. | −50 | +450 | −50 | +40 |
| 46. | −20 | +430 | −20 | +20 |
| 47. | −100 | +330 | −100 | −80 |
| 48. | −40 | +290 | −40 | −120 |
| 49. | +390 | +680 | +1,280 | +1,160 |
| 50. | −60 | +620 | −60 | +1,100 |
| 51. | −110 | +510 | −110 | +990 |
| 52. | +20 | +530 | +140 | +1,330 |
| 53. | +160 | +690 | +460 | +1,590 |
| 54. | +10 | +700 | +10 | +1,600 |
| 55. | +50 | +750 | +50 | +1,650 |
| 56. | +40 | +790 | −150 | +1,500 |
| 57. | +100 | +890 | +100 | +1,600 |
| 58. | +80 | +970 | +80 | +1,680 |
| 59. | −40 | +930 | −40 | +1,640 |
| 60. | −60 | +870 | −60 | +1,580 |
| 61. | +50 | +920 | +50 | +1,630 |
| 62. | −90 | +830 | −90 | +1,540 |
| 63. | +20 | +850 | +20 | +1,560 |

| SHOE # | FLAT BETTOR | RUNNING TOTAL | CARD COUNTER | RUNNING TOTAL |
|---|---|---|---|---|
| 64. | −120 | +730 | −120 | +1,440 |
| 65. | −100 | +630 | −100 | +1,340 |
| 66. | −40 | +590 | −40 | +1,300 |
| 67. | −10 | +580 | −10 | +1,290 |
| 68. | −100 | +480 | −100 | +1,190 |
| 69. | −60 | +420 | −60 | +1,130 |
| 70. | −140 | +280 | −140 | +990 |
| 71. | −170 | +110 | −170 | +820 |
| 72. | −20 | +90 | −20 | +800 |
| 73. | −60 | +30 | −60 | +740 |
| 74. | +110 | +140 | −410 | +330 |
| 75. | −30 | +110 | −30 | +300 |
| 76. | +160 | +270 | +160 | +460 |
| 77. | +150 | +420 | +150 | +610 |
| 78. | +140 | +560 | +140 | +750 |
| 79. | −160 | +400 | −160 | +590 |
| 80. | −100 | +300 | −100 | +490 |
| 81. | +100 | +400 | +100 | +590 |
| 82. | −80 | +320 | −80 | +510 |
| 83. | +100 | +420 | +100 | +610 |
| 84. | +70 | +490 | +70 | +680 |
| 85. | 0 | +490 | 0 | +680 |
| 86. | −40 | +450 | −40 | +640 |
| 87. | −60 | +390 | −60 | +580 |
| 88. | +140 | +530 | +140 | +720 |
| 89. | −110 | +420 | −110 | +610 |
| 90. | 0 | +420 | 0 | +610 |
| 91. | +260 | +680 | +520 | +1,130 |
| 92. | +80 | +760 | −100 | +1,030 |
| 93. | +120 | +880 | +120 | +1,150 |
| 94. | +130 | +1,010 | 0 | +1,150 |
| 95. | −80 | +930 | −80 | +1,070 |
| 96. | −50 | +880 | −50 | +1,020 |
| 97. | −60 | +820 | −60 | +960 |
| 98. | +20 | +840 | +40 | +1,000 |
| 99. | +280 | +1,120 | +460 | +1,460 |

| 100. | −80 | +1,040 | −80 | +1,380 |
|------|------|--------|------|--------|
| 101. | −120 | +920 | −120 | +1,260 |
| 102. | +140 | +1,060 | +140 | +1,400 |
| Net Totals: | | $+1,060 | | $+1,400 |

The results of these tabulations are provocative, to say the least! By using the same Quit Point strategy employed by the Positive Progressive bettor, our flat bettor went from a $610 loser to a $1,060 winner, and our card counter went from a $540 loser to a $1,400 winner!

As you may recall, our Positive Progressive bettor went from a $30 loser to a $1,890 winner, AND HIS PROFITS EXCEEDED THOSE OF THE OTHER TWO PLAYERS!

In an earlier chapter we looked at "running totals" to determine how often a player could quit play at the end of a shoe with some of the casino's money in his pocket. A review of the preceding chart reveals the following:

1. Without using Quit Point strategy, the flat bettor was ahead of the casino at the end of five out of 102 shoes. With Quit Point strategy, the flat bettor was ahead of the casino at the end of 93 out of 102 shoes.

2. Without using Quit Point strategy, the card counter was ahead of the casino at the end of 23 out of 102 shoes. With Quit Point strategy, the card counter was ahead of the casino at the end of 76 out of 102 shoes.

3. Without using Quit Point strategy, the progressive bettor was ahead of the casino at the end of 26 out of 102 shoes. With Quit Point strategy, the progressive bettor was ahead of the casino at the end of 94 out of 102 shoes — about 93% of the time!

In an earlier chapter we also discussed bankroll requirements — the amount of cash each type of player needed to survive losing periods. A comparison of bankroll requirements for our players is as follows:

1. The flat bettor who didn't use Quit Point strategy required a bankroll of $1,710 to survive losing periods. When Quit Points were employed, the bankroll required DROPPED TO $380.

2. The card counter who didn't use Quit Point strategy required a bankroll of $3,640 to survive losing periods. When Quit Points were employed, the bankroll required DROPPED TO $570.

3. The progressive bettor who didn't use Quit Point strategy required a bankroll of $1,425 to survive losing periods. When Quit Points were employed, the bankroll required DROPPED TO $510.

In all three cases the players required a MUCH SMALLER BANKROLL when the Quit Point strategy was used.

In answer to the previous question: QUIT POINT STRATEGY APPEARS TO BE VERY BENEFICIAL TO EVERY TYPE OF PLAYER.

The obvious question you should now be asking is, "Why does this strategy work?"

My answer is "I DON'T EXACTLY KNOW WHY!!!" Perhaps it's because losing shoes for the player continue to be losing shoes for the player until they are concluded. Several studies have suggested that this is true.

Perhaps it's because negative swings in good fortune continue to be negative until a shoe is concluded.

Maybe it's because some shoes favor the

dealer, and by quitting play in mid-shoe the player has more opportunities to find winning shoes at other tables.

Maybe it's because "trends" are a commonplace occurrence, and avoiding losing trends by quitting play leads to the probability of experiencing a higher percentage of winning trends.

Maybe it's because "leaning into punches" is a dumb thing to do, no matter what game you're playing!

Eventually someone more clever than I will determine why Quit Points work. Until then, accept the results illustrated in our 5,000 hands of play, accept the results of "field tests" presented in a later chapter of this book, accept the results of additional independent studies conducted by other gaming experts which are also presented in a later chapter, and enjoy the profits that accrue as a result of your use of this most beneficial twist in Positive Progressive betting strategy.

The astute reader can see that there is one "down side" to the Quit Point strategy. Since the player is required to quit play and move to a new table or wait for the start of a new shoe, a lot of playing time can be lost. If you're playing in a busy casino during peak hours, you may have to wait to find a seat at a new table. If you reach a quit point early in the dealing of a shoe, the dealer or the pit boss may not allow you to wait for the start of a new shoe. Different ways to avoid this potential "down time" will be presented in a later chapter of this book.

One conclusion is obvious, based upon the initial 5,000 hands of play: Quit points changed our progressive bettor from a $30 loser into a

$1,890 winner, and his financial gain was superior to the other two players!

In the next chapter we take a closer look at our different types of bettors, and why they choose to bet as they do.

# Chapter Twelve
# TYPES OF BLACKJACK PLAYERS

There are essentially four different types of blackjack players. Three types have much in common because they usually employ Basic Strategy and follow a betting pattern consistent with their chosen philosophy. These types are the ones discussed in this book: the Flat Bettor, the Progressive Bettor, and the Card Counter.

The fourth type, the "Inspirational Bettor," is not included in our study for reasons that will become obvious.

A general stereotyped description of each type of player is presented below:

1. The Inspirational Bettor.

This player may be a novice at the game or may have been playing for years. He may know nothing about the game or he may be well versed in blackjack theory. He may be a red chip ($5) player or a "high roller," betting hundreds of dollars on every hand.

But all inspirational bettors have one thing in common: They ignore Basic Strategy and theory — the rational aspects of the game — and allow their "gut feelings" and their ego to dictate their playing tactics. They truly believe that they can outwit the casino with inspired play; their "feel" for the game controls their wagering and playing decisions. They scoff at traditional play, are critical of people who choose a more pragmatic playing philosophy, think that books about blackjack are written by people who work for the casinos, and are convinced that their "seat of the pants" methods give them a big edge. If they lose, it's only due to bad luck, or the dealer is cheating.

This type of player is in the minority, but I've talked to many of them over the years, especially in areas where casino gaming has recently been introduced.

Occasionally this player has big winning sessions, lending credence to his style of play, but these sessions are few and far between.

Prognosis for success: Very poor. The mathematics of blackjack are extremely consistent, and emotional or irrational play will not alter the long-term results.

In terms of our analysis, it's impossible to include the inspirational bettor, since his actions are totally inconsistent and obviously can't be compared to the other three types of bettors.

2. The Flat Bettor.

The flat bettor is usually a novice player. He plays for recreation only, works with a very limited bankroll, and lacks the confidence in his game to bet more than the minimum table limit required.

Over time he learns something about Basic Strategy, usually from other players or the dealers, but may fail to apply it because an additional bet(s) might be required on double downs or splits.

Theoretically a flat bettor who uses *perfect* Basic Strategy can reduce the house advantage to one-half percent, but my opinion is that most players, regardless of betting preference, *don't play perfect Basic Strategy and further handicap themselves.*

Prognosis: Poor. The built-in house advantage of one-half percent will eventually take its toll on the flat bettor, even if perfect Basic Strategy is employed. He may have many winning sessions, but these will be offset by a higher number of losing sessions. He has no long-term chance of winning.

3. The Card Counter.

The *flawless* card counter has traditionally been identified as the only blackjack player who is capable of gaining a long-term advantage over the casino. This advantage is dependent upon the casino offering excellent gaming rules and playing conditions, and requires that the counter be skilled enough to avoid detection and possible restriction or ejection.

The state of Nevada classifies casinos as "private clubs," and allows management to disallow play by anyone suspected of being a card counter. Other gaming jurisdictions, including Atlantic City, can legally alter gaming conditions in such a way as to make card counting totally ineffectual. Casino "counter measures," such as shuffling the deck after each hand, cutting out 50% of a six-deck shoe, and limiting the maximum bet allowed are commonplace ways of eliminating the benefits of card counting.

Due to these and many other possible restrictions, and due to the skill level necessary and bankroll required to survive "short-term fluctuations in long-term probability," a very serious dedication to the task at hand is required.

Prognosis: Fair to good, depending . . . Conditions that are favorable to the card counter are critical to his long-term success, and since casino managers have access to the same information as the general public they are very successful at changing rules and altering the game in ways that limit the counter's chances of winning.

Casino gaming experts estimate that there about 300 to 3,000 "successful" card counters operating in the United States at any one time — a very small portion of the millions of people who play this game. The people who can successfully use this system of play are few and far between.

4. The Progressive Bettor.

This blackjack player is *the most common and the least researched type that exists!* Generally speaking, the majority of experienced players follow Basic Strategy and increase or decrease their bets based on some form of progression — be it negative or positive (more on this later).

The progressive bettor has usually had some experience playing the game, and has a better understanding of strategy and a larger bankroll than the flat bettor. At the same time he lacks the desire or the physiological capabilities to commit himself to the rigors of card counting.

Prognosis: Prior to the research included in this book, the general consensus of opinion among gaming experts was that most progressive betting systems won't hurt you, but they also won't help you. The statisticians claim that you will eventually suffer the same losses as the flat bettor.

As a result of this study there is considerable evidence that suggests that positive progressive betting is an excellent option for most recreational blackjack players.

My personal opinion is that positive progressive betting is the *only* reasonable option available to the recreational player.

Prior to completing the study and offering conclusions and playing recommendations, I felt it necessary that we conduct several "field tests" — applications of the betting systems in real casino environments. The next chapter describes these real-life tests.

I also felt that additional studies should be conducted to verify or refute the results of previous findings. These studies are described in the following chapter.

# Chapter Thirteen
# PROGRESSIVE BETTING FIELD TESTS

Although I've been successfully using a positive progressive betting system for several years, my method of progression is not exactly like the $20-$50 single-hand system that we used in our 5,000-hand analysis.

In order to verify the results indicated in our simulation, I conducted several field tests — the application of the $20 to $50 progression in real casinos.

The principle reasons for conducting these tests were to compare the win/loss results of a flat bettor and a progressive bettor, and to see if our progressive bettor made money using the $20 to $50 progression.

The first test occurred aboard *SeaEscape*, a 1,000+ passenger casino cruise ship that departs from Ft. Lauderdale, Florida, on "cruises to nowhere" on a daily basis. Florida currently disallows casino gaming, but has no control over vessels that travel into international waters. This ship has more than 20 blackjack tables, and game rules that are similar to those used in our simulated game. (One exception: The dealer hits soft 17, which adds a .21% advantage for the house.) Surrender is allowed, but was not applied in order to keep the field test as pure as possible.

In order to play as many hands as possible

during the five-hour cruise (about four hours of playing time), I decided to play two separate hands, each with an initial bankroll of $1,000. In effect, two players were playing the same progressive system against the same dealer at the same table.

To authenticate the test, I asked Mr. Steve Bourie, author of *American Casino Guide* and contributor to *The Experts' Guide to Casino Games,* to accompany me on the cruise and record the results of play. Mr. Bourie is a card counter and a long-time skeptic of my betting systems, so he seemed a logical choice to oversee the authenticity of this test.

Since Steve's assistance required that he carry a clipboard and write down the result of each hand played, I contacted the casino manager and explained what I was planning to do. He had no objection to our field test as long as our actions did nothing to disrupt the normal flow of the game.

This initial test took about two hours of playing time, and involved participation in 13 complete six-deck shoes. The win/loss totals for each player for each shoe are listed below:

## PROGRESSIVE BETTING FIELD TEST #1
### *SEAESCAPE,* AUGUST, 1998

| Shoe # | Player 1 | Hands Played | | Player 2 | Hands Played | |
|---|---|---|---|---|---|---|
| 1. | $ –50 | 6 | Q | $ –80 | 4 | Q |
| 2. | +570 | 15 | | –0– | 15 | |
| 3. | –150 | 9 | Q | –70 | 9 | Q |
| 4. | +80 | 10 | | –70 | 10 | |
| 5. | –120 | 12 | | +100 | 12 | |
| 6. | –80 | 9 | | +95 | 9 | |
| 7. | –110 | 12 | | –80 | 4 | Q |

| Shoe # | Player 1 | Hands Played | Player 2 | Hands Played |
|--------|----------|--------------|----------|--------------|
| 8. | +110 | 14 | –60 | 10 Q |
| 9. | +145. | 12 | +60 | 12 |
| 10. | –30 | 10 | –80 | 4 Q |
| 11. | +20 | 9 | +10 | 9 |
| 12. | –110 | 9 | –90 | 9 |
| 13. | –20 | 8 | –70 | 8 |
| Totals: | $+255 | 135 | $–335 | 115 |

Net Result: $–80   Q: Players stop play after four con-
secutive losses.

And how did our flat bettors do with the
same hands, win/loss results, and a $20 flat bet?

## FLAT BETTORS
## FIELD TEST #1

| SHOE # | PLAYER 1 | PLAYER 2 |
|--------|----------|----------|
| 1. | $ –50 | $ –80 |
| 2. | +240 | +30 |
| 3. | –140 | –80 |
| 4. | +70 | –40 |
| 5. | –100 | +40 |
| 6. | –40 | +80 |
| 7. | –100 | –80 |
| 8. | +70 | –40 |
| 9. | +110 | +80 |
| 10. | –0– | –80 |
| 11. | +20 | –20 |
| 12. | –90 | –80 |
| 13. | –0– | –50 |
| Totals: | $ –10 | $ –320 |

Net Result:  $ –330

107

Although this first field test was very limited in duration, several factors emerged which could seriously alter the effectiveness of progressive betting systems:

1. Number of hands played.

In our 5,000-hand simulation the progressive bettor played about 50 hands per shoe because he was playing a single hand against the dealer in a head-to-head contest, and the dealer dealt five decks from a six-deck shoe.

In our field test, I played two independent hands, and there were three to five other players at the same table. Also, the dealer only dealt about 70% of the cards from each shoe before reshuffling.

Consequently, due to the number of additional players and the poor deck penetration, the pace of the game was much slower, the number of hands dealt to the progressive bettor was much smaller, and the chances of being dealt consecutive winning "runs" were greatly reduced.

2. Effects of playing two hands.

It was my assumption that there would be a similarity between the end-of-shoe results for two players using the same progressive system against the same dealer.

This first field test refutes this assumption. There seems to be no similarity between the results achieved by the two players. Perhaps a longer period of play would reveal different outcomes.

3. Frequency of "runs."

As indicated earlier, all play for either player was discontinued until the next shoe if either player experienced four consecutive losses. There was no way to measure what would have happened had the player continued playing until the end of the shoe. Therefore this field test was incapable of verifying the results of "quit point" analysis that was included in our 5,000-hand simulation.

One interesting "run" did occur during Shoe #2 of this field test: Player #1 *won 11 consecutive hands in a row!* Eleven hands in a row occurred only once during our 5,000-hand analysis.

Overall conclusions and recommendations for play will be covered in a later chapter, but one fact is evident: The progressive bettors collectively lost $80, and the flat bettors collectively lost $330 *—over four times as much as the progressive bettors!* The progressive players once again fared better than the flat bettors.

## FIELD TEST #2

The second "live" testing of our $20-$50 progressive system took place in September 1998, once again on the *SeaEscape* casino ship.

The objectives of this session were slightly different than the previous test. Along with comparing progressive bettor results with flat bettor results, I also wanted to measure the effects of playing several hands against the same dealer's hand. I also planned to play at a table that had no more than one additional player, allowing more hands to be dealt per shoe. We managed to accomplish these goals for 10 consecutive shoes (about two hours of play.)

I played one hand. Steve Bourie played another hand, and recorded the results of play. Tex Tracy, a friend and novice blackjack player, played the third hand, using his own personal bankroll. We checked each other's play to insure that perfect

Basic Strategy and the betting progression were properly applied.

"Quit points" were honored throughout this field test. Whenever a player lost four consecutive hands, he discontinued play until a new shoe began.

The end-of-shoe net result for each progressive bettor is listed below, along with the results that flat bettors would have experienced:

## Field Test #2
## Summary of Progressive and Flat Bettor Results

| Shoe # | Hand #1 | | Hand #2 | | Hand #3 | |
|---|---|---|---|---|---|---|
| | **Prog.** | **Flat** | **Prog.** | **Flat** | **Prog.** | **Flat** |
| 1. | $-60 | $-60 | $-90 | $-50 | $-40 | $-40 |
| 2. | +235 | +110 | -110 | -80 | -15 | +20 |
| 3. | -120 | -120 | -20 | -0- | -115 | -70 |
| 4. | +195 | +110 | +215 | +140 | -130 | -100 |
| 5. | -80 | -40 | -40 | -0- | +25 | +40 |
| 6. | -90 | -80 | -70 | -60 | +200 | +150 |
| 7. | +90 | +110 | +70 | +60 | +40 | +20 |
| 8. | +110 | +120 | -0- | +20 | +70 | +70 |
| 9. | +200 | +80 | +95 | +60 | -70 | -60 |
| 10. | +50 | +60 | -10 | -0- | -70 | -60 |
| Totals: | $+530 | $+290 | $+40 | $+90 | $-105 | $-30 |

Note: The results for the flat bettor were obtained by calculating the win/loss totals with an initial bet of $20 — the same method used in the 5,000 hand analysis.

Total Bets: 345
Total Winning Bets: 169 (49%)
Total Losing Bets: 162 (47%)
Total Pushes: 14 (4%)
Total Player Blackjacks: 21

Total Wins and Losses Per Hand:

| Hand #1 | | Hand #2 | | Hand #3 | |
|---|---|---|---|---|---|
| Win | Loss | Win | Loss | Win | Loss |
| 61 | 50 | 58 | 56 | 50 | 56 |

Net Three-Hand Progressive Bettor Result: $+465
Net Three-Hand Flat Bettor Result: $+350

Several observations regarding this field test:

1. Even though all of our players faced the same dealer hands, the final results for each progressive bettor were quite different. Player #1 won $530, Player #2 won $40, and Player #3 lost $105.

2. The flat bettors also experienced very different outcomes, with Player #1 winning $290, Player #2 winning $90, and Player #3 losing $30. Obviously the fact that all players faced the same dealer hands was less important than the quality of each player's individual hands.

3. Once again, the total results for the progressive players was superior to the results achieved by the flat bettors, as our progressive players won $115 more than the flat bettors.

4. Our players all won a higher percentage of bets than is normal in the long run. Since the percentage of winning bets (49%) was higher than the percentage of losing bets (47%) it was inevitable that our three flat bettors would show a net profit. The progressive bettors won more than the flat bettors because of *the order in which the winning bets occurred.*

For instance, during the play of the second shoe the progressive bettor won $125 more than the flat bettor because he won seven consecutive bets, and during the play of the ninth shoe he won $120 more than the flat bettor because he again won seven consecutive bets.

5. Evidence regarding the effects of quit points is not available in this test because play was discontinued after four consecutive losses, whereas in the 5,000-hand simulation the shoe was played to conclusion in order to measure the effects of quit points. It's interesting to note that winning bets exceeded losing bets, which could have been a result of quit points or could have been a natural "positive fluctuation" in favor of the player.

6. Our novice player, Tex Tracy, was playing blackjack in a casino for the first time in his life. We continued playing for two additional hours, and he ended up with a net profit of $180! He told me that he was considering playing the game as a primary source of income. I told him that this was probably not the best course of action to take at this point in his blackjack career!

## FIELD TEST #3

In order to test our progressive betting system with gaming rules different than those used on *SeaEscape*, we decided to conduct our third field test aboard *SunCruz*, an ultra-modern casino ship that departs on "cruises to nowhere" on a daily basis from Hollywood, Florida. This vessel deals blackjack from an eight-deck shoe, and the dealer stands on soft 17, whereas *SeaEscape* employs a six-deck shoe and the dealer hits soft 17.

Our party consisted of myself, Steve Bourie (who played one hand and recorded all win/loss results,) and Lee Skelton, a friend of mine who has been learning the game and using my betting system. Incidentally, this was Lee's fifth blackjack session with me. He won on three out of four of the previous sessions, and was well ahead of the game.

Prior to the start of play we selected three seats at the same table, and told the pit boss that Steve would be recording our win/loss record and that we would in no way interfere with the flow of the game. I explained that I was doing a study of progressive and flat betting for a book that I was writing — the same information that I had presented to casino personnel on *SeaEscape*. The pit boss had no objections.

Once we entered international waters (three miles off the east coast of Florida) the casino opened and we began play. At the completion of the first hand, Steve unobtrusively wrote down our results in a 3" × 5" tablet. And then our problems began.

The pit boss, the same one who previously told us he had no objections to our plans, told Steve that he wasn't allowed to write down the results of play. I asked him why, and he told me that it was "against company policy," and that the casino manager had instructed him to inform us so.

I asked to speak to the casino manager, who promptly appeared at my side. He, Mr. Dan Snowden, told me that "company policy does not allow players to record their win/loss results." I explained what we were doing, and showed him that Steve was simply writing down wins, losses, or pushes for each hand played, and that we were in no way affecting the flow of the game. He once again told me that we couldn't do it.

We accepted his decision, as unreasonable as it seemed, but decided to continue playing without recording the results. After all, we all like black-jack!

Forty-five minutes later, I was the recipient of the most blatant form of casino harassment that I've ever experienced in my 30 years of casino gambling.

All of us were playing at the same $10 mini-mum-bet table. Steve and Lee were playing a $10 to $25 progression, and I was playing a two-hand $20 to $50 progression. As you know by now, I'm a total believer in perfect Basic Strategy. I keep a Basic Strategy card in my shirt pocket, and occa-sionally refer to it to reassure myself that I'm mak-ing the correct playing decision. I always refer to the card long before it's my turn to play, and never delay the speed of the game.

Mr. Snowden, the casino manager, was standing in our pit when I pulled the card from my pocket to verify a pending double-down on a soft hand. Mr. Snowden said, "You can't do that!"

I realized that he was talking to me and said, "Do what?"

He replied, "You can't look at that card while you're playing!"

I said, "What do you mean? It's just a Basic Strategy Card."

He said, "I know what it is, and you can't use it."

I said, "Let me be sure I understand you. You're telling me that I can't sit in this chair and look at a piece of paper?"

He replied, "That's absolutely correct, sir! You have to memorize it, like I did!"

I said, "That's it! I quit! Color me up." He seemed pleased by my decision.

Lee Skelton, my gambling buddy, also

stopped playing. He truly needed to refer to his Basic Strategy card since he hadn't memorized it, not to mention the principle at issue. Lee was a top-rated player on *SunCruz* (his favorite game had been Caribbean Stud until I introduced him to blackjack). He handed his player's rating card to Mr. Snowden and told him to destroy it since he would never be back. Mr. Snowden said, "Thank you, sir."

After we left, Steve continued to play for a few more minutes, and asked Mr. Snowden why a player couldn't look at a Basic Strategy card if it didn't distract the other players and didn't slow down the game. He repeated, "It's company policy."

Steve, Lee, and I spent the next two hours playing 25-cent video poker, waiting for the ship to return to port so we could leave.

So how did we do, in spite of casino "heat?" All three of us won money from playing blackjack, and we left the ship with over $300 in profits for less than an hour's playing time.

Unfortunately, we weren't able to compare flat and progressive betting since we weren't allowed to record the consecutive win/loss results.

Frankly, I was amazed by what had occurred. I've played blackjack and displayed a Basic Strategy card in more than 100 casinos throughout the United States, and this was the first time I was ever harassed by casino personnel.

As a follow-up, I sent a letter to the owner of this ship. I explained that I was a writer of casino gaming books, and included the preceding information which I told him would be included in my next book.

No response after three weeks. I called him

and spoke to his secretary, who told me that they had received the letter but had not had the opportunity to speak to the casino manager regarding the incident. She promised to "get back to me" within a few days. She never did.

Could it be that the casino was concerned about a potential loss? Six weeks prior to this field test, I played on *SunCruz* and enjoyed one of the best series of winning shoes that I have ever experienced. Is it possible that the casino manager remembered my previous visit and wanted to prevent a possible reoccurrence? If this is the case, I may be the first progressive bettor that's ever been perceived as a threat to a casino! I think I'm honored!

It's more likely that the casino manager for this ship simply doesn't want players to know how to properly play blackjack — a very narrow-minded attitude that doesn't bode well for the future of this company.

Since this incident occurred, I've continued to receive offers in the mail from *SunCruz* regarding special events only available to "preferred customers." Interesting . . .

This concludes the field tests of our 5,000-hand analysis. Our progressive bettors showed more positive results than the flat bettors for the first two sessions, and all three progressive bettors made money on the third session.

# Chapter Fourteen
# ADDITIONAL STUDIES

In order to further verify (or possibly refute) the conclusions drawn from the 5,000 hands of play that are the focal point of this book, several casino gaming experts, including Fred Renzey, conducted independent "reenactments" of the study.

Fred Renzey manually dealt and played 1,004 hands. He made a few changes in the game plan in order to equalize the average amount wagered on each hand by each type of player, and he used a much more sophisticated card counting system.

During this particular "run," the flat bettor wagered $30 per hand (rather than $20) and the card counter used a $15 to $180 bet spread (rather than a $20 to $240 bet spread.) The progressive bettor continued to use a $20 to $50 progression. Fred felt that equalizing the average amount wagered might change the overall outcome.

As the following chart indicates, this was not the case.

## RUNNING TOTALS —
## END OF SHOE RESULTS

| Shoe # | Flat Bettor | Card Counter | Progressive Bettor |
|---|---|---|---|
| 1. | $ −180 | $ −120 | $ −130 |
| 2. | −150 | −112.50 | −155 |
| 3. | −690 | −412.50 | −605 |

| Shoe # | Flat Bettor | Card Counter | Progressive Bettor |
|---|---|---|---|
| 4. | –720 | –412.50 | –575 |
| 5. | –1,425 | –742.50 | –1,080 |
| 6. | –1,845 | –967 | –1,435 |
| 7. | –1,715 | –630 | –1,490 |
| 8. | –2,540 | –3,712.50 | –2,150 |
| 9. | –2,495 | –3,690.50 | –2,120 |
| 10. | –2,750 | –3,732.50 | –2,300 |
| 11. | –2,750 | –3,732.50 | –2,240 |
| 12. | –2,540 | –3,567.50 | –2,110 |
| 13. | –2,555 | –3,575 | –2,215 |
| 14. | –2,765 | –3,605 | –2,125 |
| 15. | –2,675 | –3,560 | –2,005 |
| 16. | –2,315 | –2,900 | –1,630 |
| 17. | –2,570 | –4,062.50 | –1,840 |
| 18. | –3,110 | –4,347.50 | –2,260 |
| 19. | –2,960 | –4,272.50 | –2,310 |
| 20. | –3,125 | –4,580 | –2,420 |
| 21. | –3,440 | –5,300 | –2,765 |

Note: The preceding 21 shoes were extremely negative from the players' standpoint. About 58% of the bets were losers.

But, once again, the positive progressive bettor had the best results, losing $680 less than the flat bettor and $1,535 less than the card counter!

Another blackjack expert, a card counter who uses the name "Bootlegger" agreed to participate in this project. Bootlegger chooses not to have his true identity revealed because he's a serious player and doesn't want his name known to casino operators. Initially a hi-lo counter, for the last 16 months he's logged 265 hours of play using the KO system devised by Olaf Vancura and Ken Fuchs (*Knockout Blackjack*, Huntington Press, 1988). He reports profits of "more than 1,000 units" and won 65% of the sessions he played.

Bootlegger graciously agreed to manually play 1,000 hands which compared the results of Positive Progressive betting, flat betting, and KO system card counting. He applied the same game rules, strategies, and conditions used in the other trials in this book. His results of play are as follows:

OVERALL SUMMARY
Shoes Played: 21
Hands Played: 1,011
Winning Hands: 432
Losing Hands: 497
Pushes: 82
Winning Bets: 486 (48%)
Losing Bets: 545 (52%)
Total Bets (Excluding Pushes): 1,031
Player Blackjacks: 47
Dealer Blackjacks: 40

FINANCIAL RESULTS OF PLAY
The Positive Progressive Bettor ($20 to $50)
lost $410
The Flat Bettor ($20 per bet) lost $740
The Flat Bettor ($30 per bet) lost $1,110
The KO Counter ($20 to $240) lost $430

Again, for the sake of brevity, the charts depicting the above results have not been included in this book, but are available to interested readers upon request. My mailing address is included at the conclusion of this book.

Three other aspects of the game were analyzed on the basis of this 1,011 hands of play:

## 1. END-OF-SHOE RESULTS.

The Positive Progressive Bettor was financially ahead of the casino at the end of 11 of 21 shoes.

The $20 Flat Bettor was ahead of the casino for one of 21 shoes.

The $30 Flat Bettor was ahead of the casino for one of 21 shoes.

The KO Counter was ahead of the casino for 15 of 21 shoes.

In other words, the KO counter and the Positive Progressive Bettor could have quit the game with casino money in their pockets 72% or 53% of the time, respectively, whereas the Flat Bettors were never ahead of the casino after the first shoe played. Obviously, I'd rather be a KO Counter or a Positive Progressive Bettor!

## 2. CONSECUTIVE WINS AND LOSSES.

In order to measure the effects of clusters of winning or losing hands, I reviewed the 21 shoes of play and recorded the number of times our players won or lost five or more consecutive hands.

There were nine occasions when the player, regardless of his betting style, won five or more consecutive bets, and 16 occasions when the player lost five or more consecutive hands. These results are not representative of long-term expectations, since the statisticians tell us that a player is expected to have almost as many winning clusters as losing clusters.

How did these disproportional results affect the financial outcome of the Positive Progressive Bettor and the $30 Flat Bettor? To answer this question I calculated the amount won or lost for each cluster by each player, and found that the

Positive Progressive Bettor lost a total of $90 and the $30 Flat Bettor lost a total of $840.

### 3. AVERAGE COUNT COMPARED TO CONSECUTIVE WINNING HANDS.

Using the data presented above, I calculated the average KO count for consecutive winning and losing clusters. Using Bootlegger's slightly modified method of recording the running count for each hand played, I discovered that the average count for clusters of consecutive winning hands was 9.89, and the average count for clusters of consecutive losing hands was 11.6. The average count was *more positive* — theoretically more advantageous to the player — during losing clusters than it was during winning clusters!

Based on the data generated from this 21-shoe sample, I reached the following conclusions:

1. As in previous studies, the positive progressive player had a track record superior to the other players.

2. As in previous studies, the positive progressive player was financially ahead of the casino much more often than the flat bet players.

3. Once again, there appears to be no relationship between the card counter's running count and the clusters of winning or losing hands.

Simply stated, Bootlegger's 21-shoe "run" showed results that are totally consistent with all previous studies presented in this text.

Another casino gaming expert who read the initial manuscript of this book suggested that the simplified card counting system employed in the 5,000 hands of play was inadequate, and may have accounted for the card counter's lack of success.

As a result of this constructive criticism, I played 20 shoes of blackjack using a more advanced counting system — Fred Renzey's "Up-Graded Black Ace Count" strategy, which carries a 93% efficiency for betting purposes. The 20-shoe "run" resulted in 991 hands played and 1,101 bets placed on the table.

Unlike previous studies, our players experienced potentially positive results. They won 45.5% of the bets, lost 45.5% of the bets, and pushed on 9% of the bets. They also drew six more blackjacks than the dealer.

I constructed several charts which are similar to those used in previous chapters of this book, but decided that it would be redundant to include them at this point.

The following data summarizes the 20-shoe session:

    1. Overall Results:
        Shoes Played: 20
        Hands Played: 991
        Bets Placed: 1,101
        Bets Won: 498 (45.5%)
        Bets Lost: 501 (45.5%)
        Bets Pushed: 102 (9%)
        Player Blackjacks: 49
        Dealer Blackjacks: 43
    2. Results Of Play:
        Flat Bettor Won $430
        Progressive Bettor Won $830.00
        Card Counter Lost $500.00
    3. Conclusions:

In spite of the up-graded counting system, the card counter was the only player that lost money. This was caused by an *incredibly* bad shoe (#14 in the session) that resulted in a $2,820 loss, although the count was very positive (ranging from

+20 to +40) for 37 of the 46 hands dealt from this shoe.

The flat bettor won almost as many bets as he lost, and won a total of $430 as a result of the extra $10 gained on each of the three to two pay-offs received from his blackjack hands.

The Positive Progressive Bettor won $830, almost twice as much as the flat bettor, as a result of his betting style. Once again, the overall pattern was not altered due to a change in the rules. Win, lose, or draw, the positive progressive bettor was once again more successful than the other players.

Another study was conducted due to a conversation with a friend who has an interest in the game, and read parts of the initial manuscript of this book. He plays blackjack on his personal computer, and asked me if he could practice using my Positive Progressive system with his blackjack software, and would the results of play be the same as the manually-dealt game referred to in this book.

To answer his questions, I borrowed his computer game and played 20 shoes of blackjack. This game, entitled *Wizard Works Windows Blackjack* (Wizard Ware, Inc., 1450 Concordia Avenue, St. Paul, MN 55104), allows the player to pre-program the rules of the game. It also allows the computer to play the player's hand using the same Basic Strategy used in this book, eliminating the possibility of a misplay in Basic that could occur with the manually-dealt game.

Therefore, I selected a six-deck game with 75% penetration, head-to-head play, and the same game rules and Basic Strategy employed throughout this book. My only task was to record the win/loss/push results, and then compare flat betting to Positive Progressive betting. My progressive bettor employed the same $20-$50 spread, and I analyzed the results of the flat bettor who bet either $20 or $30 per hand.

Once again, I've not illustrated the shoe-by-shoe results, due to my desire to eliminate redundancy and reduce the cost of this book. A summary of the 20 shoes is as follows:

Total Shoes Played: 20
Total Bets Placed: 962
Total % of Bets Won: .43
Total % of Bets Lost: .46
Total % of Bets Pushed: .11
Net Result of Play:
> Positive Progressive Bettor: Won $90
> Flat Bettor ($20 per Bet): Lost $80
> Flat Bettor ($30 per Bet): Lost $120

Once again, the positive progressive bettor showed results superior to the flat bettor, and in this case was the only player that showed a profit, although only 43% of the hands were winners.

But what about the two casino gaming experts who reviewed *The Ultimate Blackjack Book*, my book that recommended progressive betting (see Chapter 2) and questioned the value of the concept?

Frank Scoblete, author of numerous books, videos, and cassette tapes about casino gaming — actually, the current best-selling writer in the world on the subject — wrote the introduction to this book! His decision to do so was based on his review of the manuscript and his acceptance of the credibility of my research. I don't have all the answers, but Mr. Scoblete recognizes the validity of my position.

John Grochowski, syndicated columnist for the *Chicago Sun-Times*, author of numerous casino gaming books, including *The Casino Answer Book* (Bonus Books, 1998) agreed to manually deal a few shoes of blackjack and see what transpired. He sent me the results of six shoes of play — 286 bets. The players won 46% of the bets, the dealer won 49% of the bets, and 5% of the bets were pushes. The Positive Progressive bettor ($20 to $50) lost $15, the $20 Flat bettor lost $90, and the $30 Flat bettor lost $345. As usual, the positive progressive bettor showed the best financial results from play.

I'm sure that John is not convinced that progressive betting is the best way to go with this game, but the numbers, as usual, speak for themselves.

Additional studies that compare various betting systems could go on forever. New card-counting schemes are offered several times a year, or so it seems. It's my hope that similar effort will be devoted to research that improves the quality of the progressive betting system recommended in this book.

Dr. Henry Tamburin, an astute player of the game, and author of numerous gaming books, including *Blackjack: Take the Money and Run*, had this to say about an early draft of this book: "I was impressed with your detailed study on progressive betting and surprised at the results. I'm sure that your conclusions will rekindle the controversy and spur others to take a look at it."

I hope that Henry is correct.

# Chapter Fifteen
# OTHER PROGRESSIVE BETTING SYSTEMS

The concept of progressive betting is not new. In fact, it's been around for about 300 years!

Many systems originated in Europe and were initially applied to the games of roulette and baccarat. A few that have survived to the present are:

1. Martingale. This is one of the oldest documented progressive systems, and is based on a negative progression. It's named after Henry Martingale, a London casino owner in the 1700s.

The system is very simple: If you win a bet, continue to bet the original amount. If you lose a bet, double the amount that you wagered, and keep doubling the bet until you win. You will eventually win the initial amount wagered — and show a profit. A normal Martingale progression while losing would be $5, $10, $20, $40, $80, etc. If you lost the first four bets and won the fifth bet, your net profit would be $5 (Won $80; lost $75 = +$5).

This system would be unbeatable were it not for one fact: Modern casinos place limits on how much can be bet at one time. If you are playing at a $10 minimum bet blackjack table, the normal maximum bet is $500. Your progression from an initial loss would be $20, $40, $80, $160, and $320. After six consecutive losses the next bet would

have to be $640, which would not be allowed be-
cause the table limit is $500.

In essence this system allows you to win
small amounts most of the time, but eventually will
cost you a small fortune when you hit the inevitable
losing streak.

2. Grand Martingale. This system is similar
to the Martingale, with an added twist: You double
the previous bet, *plus one unit*. Results are similar,
except that you win slightly more and reach the
table limit a bit faster.

3. Labourchere. The Labourchere system
was developed by a French mathematician in the
18th century, and made popular by an English
gambler who died in 1912. This is a "cancellation"
system, as in 1, 2, 3, 4, 5. Each number represents
units of wager. The first bet is the total of the first
and last number in the row, added together. Each
time you lose, write that number at the end of the
row. Each time you win, cross out the first and last
numbers and go to the next first and last numbers
for your next bet. Keep playing until all numbers
have been crossed out. You will win the combined
amount of the original numbers when all are can-
celed out, as in 1, 2, 3, 4, 5 = 15.

The problem is the series can climb beyond
table limits, or you will win small amounts and then
lose every bet, and restart, and lose every bet, etc.
Sound advice: Try this at home for fun, but *don't*
try this system in a casino!

4. d'Alembert. This system was also invented
by a French mathematician, based on the assumption of "equilibrium." You subtract a chip
after each winning bet, and add a chip after each
losing bet.

Again, table limits will eventually destroy

you. In the long run the system will give you lots of small winning sessions, and a few big losing sessions.

All of the above systems have two major faults: Each of them requires a bet increase after a loss (some or all of the time) and each of them is open-ended, meaning that there is no cap on the maximum amount placed at risk. Due to table limits, these systems lead to long-term losses.

Positive progressive systems, philosophically similar to the one used in our 5,000-hand analysis, have also been around for quite some time. Charles Einstein, credited with being the originator of the card counting system that became popularized as the Hi-Opt 1, authored a book entitled *Basic Blackjack Betting* in 1981. His "rhythm" system required increasing the bet while winning and decreasing the bet while losing. During the 1980s other authors published books along the same line.

Reaction from traditional card counting authors and statisticians to Mr. Einstein's book and to other books that propose progressive betting systems has always been negative. Almost without exception, those that preach the merits of card counting are totally intolerant of any other method of play and are convinced that card counting, and *only* card counting, leads to blackjack success.

In most cases the card counting advocates simply ignore other approaches to the game, or discount them by simply stating, "They don't work." In the case of Mr. Einstein, they countered his proposals with mathematical theorems and million-hand computer-generated simulations, primarily because he was "one of the flock," a card counting advocate who had the audacity to propose an alternative to card counting.

A later chapter of this book is devoted to the seemingly endless debate between those who see merit in progressive betting and those who believe that it can't possibly be beneficial.

Frankly, the "tunnel vision" attitude of these nationally-known writers has always annoyed me, and has seriously hampered my efforts to prove or disprove the validity of my method of play. I'm reminded of times past when the "experts" believed that the world was flat, when they knew for sure that the only way to cure illness was to drain blood from the body, when they were convinced that if Man were meant to fly he would have been born with wings.

I assume that this book will be ignored, or "theoretically" attacked and refuted by many traditional gaming experts. But I also assume that many who read this book will profit by applying a progressive betting system. It's up to you to decide if the world is flat or round.

# Chapter Sixteen

# A COMPARISON OF PROGRESSIVE SYSTEMS

Do all progressive systems based on increasing the bet after winning yield the same result? Not necessarily.

One of the more popular progressive betting systems in use today was proposed by Donald Dahl in his 1993 book, *Progression Blackjack*. This book sparked my interest in progressive betting, and explains much of the rationale for this type of wagering.

Mr. Dahl's system differs from the Positive Progressive system used in our study in two distinct ways: He doesn't automatically increase his bet after every win, and he recommends a longer series of "steps."

For example, he proposes the following progression when the minimum bet is $10: $10-$10-$15-$15-$20-$20-$30-$30-$50-$50-$75-$75-$100-$100. You can see that the increases are small during the early part of a winning cluster, and become more dramatic as the winning cluster continues.

As with other positive progressive systems, the player reverts to the minimum bet after a loss.

In addition, Mr. Dahl recommends "jumping" one or two steps if the player gets a blackjack or wins more than one bet due to doubles or splits.

For instance, if the player draws a blackjack, he jumps one step in the progression. If he wins a double-down, he jumps two steps unless he will be risking more than he won on the previous hand, in which case he would only jump one step. For a more thorough description of this system, read his book. I highly recommend it!

In order to compare this system to the one used in our study, I applied it to the first 20 shoes (968 bets) of our 5,000 hands of play. The shoe-by-shoe results for each type of system bettor are presented below:

## DAHL SYSTEM VS. POSITIVE PROGRESSIVE SYSTEM END OF SHOE RESULTS

| SHOE # | DAHL | POSITIVE PROGRESSIVE |
|:------:|:----:|:--------------------:|
| 1. | $ –90 | $ –40 |
| 2. | +135 | +215 |
| 3. | –75 | –95 |
| 4. | +10 | +100 |
| 5. | –190 | –250 |
| 6. | –70 | –90 |
| 7. | –15 | –35 |
| 8. | +45 | +40 |
| 9. | –145 | –165 |
| 10. | +220 | +230 |
| 11. | –150 | –215 |
| 12. | +45 | +65 |
| 13. | –110 | –115 |
| 14. | –170 | –150 |
| 15. | +85 | +40 |
| 16. | –100 | –120 |
| 17. | –200 | –135 |
| 18. | –190 | –250 |
| 19. | –05 | +175 |

| SHOE # | DAHL | POSITIVE PROGRESSIVE |
|---|---|---|
| 20. | +220 | +360 |
| TOTALS: | $ –750 | $ –435 |
| | (13 Losing Shoes, | (12 Losing Shoes, |
| | 7 Winning Shoes) | 8 Winning Shoes) |

The preceding chart shows that both players experienced more losing shoes than winning shoes, and that both players lost money.

But it's significant to note that the Positive Progressive bettor lost much less than the Dahl System bettor.

I attribute this difference to two factors:

1. It seems that the Dahl system requires long strings of consecutive winning bets to be totally effective — longer strings than required by the Positive Progressive bettor.

2. I suspect that the escalation of the bet increase in the latter steps of the Dahl System is overly optimistic. If we look at the bet *increases* that occur in his $10 progression, we get the following: $0-$10-$0-$10-$0-$10-$0-$25-$0-$25. The larger increases occur at the *probable end* of clusters of wins, rather than early in the series of wins.

Previous charts in this book clearly show that clusters of four, five, or six winning bets are much more likely to occur than clusters of eight, nine, or ten winning bets. It's my opinion that not increasing the bet in the early stages of a winning cluster hurts the potential of progressive betting, and that escalating the normal increase in the latter stages of a progression is too risky.

In all fairness to Mr. Dahl, the sample used to compare the systems is rather small, and more research is required to verify the weaknesses that I perceive.

Another well-known progressive betting system is the New York System, popularized and advocated by John Patrick, a professional gambler and prolific writer of casino gaming books.

In his book, *John Patrick's Blackjack* (Carol Publishing Group Edition, 1995) he describes the system in detail. It is essentially a "regression-progression" system, and works like this: the player starts with a two-unit bet (a unit is one chip,) where the first bet is at least twice the amount of the minimum table limit. If he wins, he *reduces* the next bet to one unit. If he wins again, he returns to the two-unit bet and continues to increase the bet after each consecutive win.

If the player were gambling at a $10 minimum bet table, his winning progression would be as follows: $20-$10-$20-$30-$30-$40-$50.

After any net loss, he reverts to the $20 bet.

Mr. Patrick also suggests that the player quit the game if he loses the *first* four hands in a shoe or deck.

He offers other variations to this plan, based on the conservative or aggressive nature of the player, but this pattern most closely resembles the systems previously analyzed and is the one selected for the next comparison.

Using Mr. Patrick's system, I played the first 20 shoes of our 5,000 hands — the same way that I played Mr. Dahl's system. The end-of-shoe totals for the New York System are presented below:

# NEW YORK SYSTEM VS. POSITIVE PROGRESSIVE SYSTEM END OF SHOE RESULTS

| SHOE # | NEW YORK | POSITIVE PROGRESSIVE |
|--------|----------|----------------------|
| 1. | $ –50 | $ –40 |
| 2. | +65 | +215 |
| 3. | –65 | –95 |
| 4. | –10 | +100 |
| 5. | –100 | –250 |
| 6. | +10 | –90 |
| 7. | +35 | –35 |
| 8. | –0– | +40 |
| 9. | –95 | –165 |
| 10. | +150 | +230 |
| 11. | –215 | –95 |
| 12. | +135 | +65 |
| 13. | –115 | –115 |
| 14. | –150 | –150 |
| 15. | +100 | +40 |
| 16. | –100 | –120 |
| 17. | –175 | –135 |
| 18. | –110 | –250 |
| 19. | –95 | +175 |
| 20. | +65 | +360 |
| Totals: | $ –720 | $ –435 |
| | (New York) | (Positive Progressive) |
| | 13 Losing Shoes | 12 Losing Shoes |
| | 7 Winning Shoes | 8 Winning Shoes |

The New York System showed a net loss of $720 — very similar to the $750 lost by the Dahl System.

A very general observation, based on this limited sample, is that Patrick's system *loses less* on shoes that show losses, but also *wins less* on shoes that are profitable to the player.

In regard to the suggestion that the player quit the game after losing the first four hands, this occurred twice during the 20 shoes of play. On Shoe #13, the New York bettor lost $100 on the first four hands. By continuing to play he eventually lost $115 on this shoe. On Shoe #19, the New York bettor lost $80 on the first four hands. By continuing to play, he lost $95 on the shoe.

Consequently, the New York bettor would have *saved* $30 in losses by quitting after the first four losses, and would have only lost $690 in 20 shoes of play — still considerably more than the $435 lost by the Positive Progressive bettor.

One more question before we move on: What would be the end-of-shoe results for the Positive Progressive bettor if the Quit Point plan for this system (quit play after four consecutive net losing bets) had been honored?

If you total the results for the first 20 shoes from the chart presented in the Quit Points chapter, you'll see that our Positive Progressive bettor would have suffered a total loss of $130, rather than the $435 that he lost by ignoring the quit point and playing through the end of the shoe.

For a more detailed explanation of the New York System, I suggest that you read Mr. Patrick's book.

One fact should be evident as a result of our comparison of betting systems: there are major differences in progressive systems, and some are better than others.

# Chapter Seventeen
# COMPUTER SIMULATIONS

As you'll recall from an early chapter of this book I explained that the studies would be based on manually-dealt play rather than computer simulated data, because I could find no existing software designed to measure the merits of progressive betting.

After completing all of the work preceding this chapter, I received a call from Dr. Henry Tamburin regarding a gentleman who had contacted him. This man, a computer software systems engineer and avid player of blackjack, had e-mailed him to ask about progressive betting, and wanted to know if there were any computer programs on the market that related to this betting method. Henry immediately recognized that this man, Mr. I. B. Winner (fictitious name, of course) and I had very similar interests, and suggested that I contact him.

I called Mr. Winner at his home in California, and learned that he was both capable of and willing to create a computer program that would compare Progressive, Flat, and Counter betting systems. He has a BS Degree in Mechanical Engineering, an MS Degree in systems engineering, and 14 years of experience in computer software technology. I also learned that he is a serious blackjack player, a "preferred customer" at many casinos, and has been a card counter since 1991. Obviously, he suffers from the same paranoia that most card counters experience — hence, the fictitious name.

Within two weeks he had created a blackjack simulation program that was capable of providing us with information about the long-term value of progressive betting.

This program compares the differences between a Positive Progressive bettor ($20 - $50), a Flat bettor ($30), and a KO Counter ($10 - $80) who all play the same hands and experience the same win/loss/push results. The program employs essentially the same format applied to all other studies in this book, except that the players are not allowed to double-down after splitting and can only split twice. Since these rule changes have the same negative effect on all three players, a comparison of overall results is unaltered.

The computer plays a series of 1,000 consecutive hands, then stops play and calculates the negative or positive percentage "edge" for each type of player. The "edge" is the total ending bankroll divided by the total units bet by each player during the 1,000 hands of play.

Each 1,000-hand "run" takes about six seconds to play — a heck of a lot faster than manually dealing the cards!

Using this program I played 200,000 hands of blackjack, and summarized the results after each 50,000 hands of play. Once again for the sake of brevity, I've not listed the totals for each 1,000-hand series, but the raw data is available to interested parties. The results are as follows:

# 50,000 HAND SUMMARIES
# TOTAL OF 200,000 HANDS

| Hands | Progressive "Edge" | Flat ($30) "Edge" | KO Count "Edge" |
|---|---|---|---|
| 1st 50,000 | + .701% | + .500% | + .479% |
| 2nd 50,000 | – .417% | – .975% | + .529% |
| 3rd 50,000 | – .161% | – .645% | – .435% |
| 4th 50,000 | – .798% | –1.043% | + .045% |
| Net Average | – .168% | – .541% | + .155% |

The preceding chart confirms the results of previous studies regarding the relationship between Positive Progressive and Flat bettors. The Positive Progressive bettor seems to *always* win more or lose less than the Flat bettor who is averaging the same amount wagered per bet.

This chart also indicates that card counters *can gain an advantage in the long run*. This fact was not evident in previous short-run studies. I attribute part of this to the fact that the KO counter's initial bet was only $10, compared to the $30 Flat bet and the average bet of about $30 by the Positive Progressive bettor. Whatever the case, the KO counter made money!

What about extremes? I always like to see what happens to players when the cards flow in a manner which is less than probable.

Frank Scoblete (*Best Blackjack*) confirms that in the long run all players will win approximately 44 and lose approximately 48 out of every 100 hands played; and about eight hands will "push."

Applying this proven statistic to our 1,000 hand runs, the players should average 440 winning hands per thousand, and the dealer should average 480 winning hands per thousand. But how are players affected by extreme fluctuations in normal results? In this case, what happens when the players win at least 460 hands per thousand, or the dealer wins at least 500 hands per thousand? Does a difference of 20 or more hands per thousand seriously alter the normal expected outcomes?

To answer this question, I played 150,000 computer-simulated consecutive hands (in sets of 1,000 hands) and recorded the results when the dealer or the player won more hands than he was expected to win. There were 29 occasions when the dealer or the player won 20 or more hands per thousand than is normal in the long run — about 20% of the 1,000-hand runs.

On only six occasions did our players win over 460 of 1,000 hands played — but they all did well! The Positive Progressive bettor averaged a + .6043% gain per 1,000 hands played, the Flat bettor gained + .6553%, and the KO counter gained + .8860%.

The dealer, on the other hand, experienced 23 occasions when he won at least 500 hands or better — extreme dealer wins outnumbered extreme player wins by almost 4 to 1 — and the players were adversely affected. The Positive Progressive bettor averaged –.6670% loss, the Flat bettor averaged -.6483% loss, and the KO counter averaged –.6954% loss.

What conclusions can we draw from these 350,000 simulated hands of play?

1. THE POSITIVE PROGRESSIVE BETTOR ONCE AGAIN WON MORE OR LOST LESS THAN THE FLAT BETTOR. The results

from the 200,000-hand simulation confirm every other study conducted in this book.

2. ALL THREE TYPES OF PLAYERS SUFFER SIMILAR LOSSES OR ENJOY SIMILAR GAINS WHEN ABNORMAL NUMBERS OF LOSSES OR WINS OCCUR. In spite of betting style, all three types of players make money during "positive" runs and lose money during "negative" runs, as indicated in the 150,000-hand simulation.

3. DON'T COMMIT YOURSELF TO A BETTING SYSTEM BASED ON SHORT-TERM PROFITS. If you had read this book, employed my Positive Progressive betting system, and experienced the +.701% "edge" gained from the first 50,000 hand summary in the 200,000-hand analysis, you could conclude that my system was amazing! OR, if you had read this book, employed my Positive Progressive betting system, and experienced the –.798% "edge" lost during the fourth 50,000-hand summary in the 200,000-hand analysis, you could conclude that my system was an absolute bust!

4. "LONG-TERM" PLAY *REALLY IS* LONG TERM! The first study in this chapter reviews the results of 200,000 hands of simulated play. I figure that a good player can average 100 hands per hour in head-to-head competition against a fast dealer. At this rate, if a player stayed at the same table for 20 hours per day, he could play 2,000 hands of non-stop blackjack, and it would take only 100 days to complete 200,000 hands of play! Although I've played blackjack for 20 hours at a time, I don't think I could maintain this pace for more than one day! Realistically, most dedicated players are good for six hours per day, and average about 80 hands per hour in head-to-

head competition, and would require more than 400 days to play 200,000 hands. That's a lot of blackjack — more than most people play in a lifetime!

My point is that it's OK to study long-term probabilities, but keep in mind that most players win or lose on the basis of short term results of play.

Several days prior to completing the manuscript of this book, Mr. Winner e-mailed me another new computer simulation program. This program is capable of playing single six-deck shoes, and then giving win/loss results for the Flat ($30) bettor, the Positive Progressive ($20 - $50) bettor, and the KO Card Counter ($10 - $120). The program also presents totals won or lost by each type of player when the "Quit Points" strategy (Chapter Eleven) is applied.

In other words, this program practically duplicates the research methodology used in my 5,000-hand study. The only differences are a few rule changes (no double-down after split, only split twice, only 75% shoe penetration) which equally affect all three players.

Using this new program, my computer played one hundred shoes of blackjack, and I recorded the amount of money won or lost by each player at the end of each shoe. The net results from these 100 shoes of play, which are presented below, lend more credence to my progressive system, and to my use of quit point strategy.

100-SHOE COMPUTER SIMULATION
Total Hands Played: 4,103
Total Hands Won: 1,976 (49%)

Total Hands Lost: 2,121 (51%)
Net Result *Without* Quit Point Strategy:
    Flat bettor won $355.
    KO counter lost $615.
    Progressive bettor won $785.
Net Result *With* Quit Point Strategy:
    Flat bettor won $2,745
    KO counter won $1,295
    Progressive bettor won $3,045

As you can see, the Positive Progressive bettor won more than the other two players, both with and without the use of the quit point strategy.

Also, the quit point strategy *dramatically improved* the financial outcome of all three types of players. In fact, by using the quit point strategy the total amount collectively gained by the players was $6,560!

As a finale to this series of computer-simulated trials, my trusty old Packard Bell 486 Computer played 2,275,851 hands of blackjack while I watched the Denver Broncos destroy the Atlanta Falcons at Super Bowl XXXIII. The total elapsed time required to run this simulation was less than four hours. Computers are amazing!

End-of-run results show that both the progressive bettor and the flat bettor lost money, partially due to win/loss percentages and player-unfriendly rules, and possibly due to no use of the quit point strategy (this option is not currently a function of this program).

The most significant result from this long-run study relates to financial outcome: the Positive Progressive bettor lost $27,610 *less* than the Flat bettor!

Mr. Winner and I continue to study the attributes and deficiencies associated with progressive betting systems, and continue to refine the quality of the programs being employed, but publication deadlines prevent further studies from being included in this book. Perhaps at a later time . . .

My primary question — and concern — is "Why hasn't anyone else developed and analyzed similar computer programs?" Mr. Winner is a very intelligent and knowledgeable technician and blackjack player, but is he the only person in the last 20 years who has had the interest and ability to address this question?

# Chapter Eighteen
# THE OPPOSITE OPINION, AND WHY IT'S WRONG!

Those of you who are not fanatical followers of the game of blackjack are probably not aware that there has been a hotly contested debate regarding the merits of progressive betting for many, many years.

Many nationally-known writers, computer experts, statisticians, and mathematicians, such as Anthony Curtis, Arnold Snyder, Stanford Wong, and Peter Griffen have studied the game and concluded that card counting is the only way to win. Coincidentally (or perhaps not) most of the experts are die-hard card counters, which predisposes them to be skeptical of any method of play which might question the possibility that alternative systems could be useful to the average player.

Card counting proponents have dominated blackjack gaming research and literature for over 25 years, and have been actively instrumental in limiting inquiry into other betting systems, by either ignoring the literature that offers other alternatives, or by refuting the efforts of those who propose betting systems other than card counting.

For example, a running debate was published in *Blackjack Forum*, a reputable newsletter edited by Arnold Snyder. Charles Einstein, originator of a respected card-counting system, published a book entitled *Basic Blackjack Betting,* and proposed a simplistic betting system called "Rhythm Betting." Einstein's method of play, suggesting that a player should bet more while winning and less while losing, *regardless of the count*, drew an immediate critical reaction from the traditional card counters.

Einstein's 71-page pamphlet, retail priced at $2, was published by GBC Press (Gambler's Book Club). His manually-dealt samples of 16,622 *consecutively-dealt* hands and 12,008 *consecutively-dealt* hands employed a betting system that required the player to start play with a $5 wager, then bet $5 after a loss and $25 after a win. Einstein writes: "I say it's simple. I say it works. I say it's hassle free." He concludes by stating that, "It has a capacity for profit that can be demonstrated."

Summarizing a two-year debate, Einstein's plan was rejected by several statisticians and computer experts, and discounted by Peter Griffen's reference to "Bayes' Theorem." In spite of Mr. Einstein's efforts to defend his position, Snyder concluded the debate by saying that this system could not work, so "case closed."

Incidentally, this debate transpired between 1982 and 1984, based on Einstein's 1980 publication.

So what did the card counters use as their justification for rejecting progressive systems?

Their total denouncement of progressive betting was (and still is) based upon the two methods of research that they employ: computer simulation, and a mathematical concept known as Bayes' Theorem.

Einstein argued that computer simulations failed to record the result of every hand played, failed to provide win/loss results for every bet placed, failed to recognize the significance of splits and double-downs, failed to record *consecutive* hands of play, and failed to record how clusters of winning and losing hands affected the player's financial outcome.

Bayes' Theorem, Einstein argued, was irrelevant, since he never claimed that progressive players *expected* to win the next hand.

I never met the man, but I totally agree with Mr. Einstein's position! I wasn't aware that this debate had occurred until *after* I conducted my initial 5,000 hands of play, analyzed the results, reached conclusions, and completed the initial draft of this book.

I obtained a copy of the book from Henry Tamburin, who possesses a very comprehensive library of casino gaming literature. Much to my surprise, most of my conclusions mirror the conclusions reached by Mr. Einstein — almost 20 years before I began my research!

So here's what I believe:

1. Most computer-generated simulation programs are incapable of judging the validity of progressive betting systems, due to faulty, incorrect, or non-existent programming. The results of *consecutive* hands of play are totally ignored. The program recently developed by my associate, Mr. I. B. Winner, is the only one I know of that attempts to compare progressive, flat, and card counting systems.

2. Bayes' Theorem, a theoretical concept, should not be used to pass judgment on empirical evidence.

Bayes' Theorem is a statistical tool suggesting that "probabilities should be revised as we acquire additional knowledge about an event." The varied applications of this theorem include its use in paternity suits to calculate the probability that a defendant is the father of a child, and also its use as a conceptual basis for the validity of card counting systems in blackjack.

The assumption made by card counting proponents is that progressive bettors *expect* to win a bet after winning the previous bet. Bayes' Theorem proves that the probability of winning a blackjack bet after winning or losing the previous bet is just as likely as losing a bet after losing or winning the previous bet. Consequently, there is no *theoretical* reason to increase the wager after a winning hand, or decrease the wager after a losing hand.

When the Theorem is applied to card counting, there *is* a theoretical reason to increase the bet if there is a disproportionately high number of face cards remaining in the deck or shoe, since high cards favor the player and the player is more likely to win as long as this disparity exists. The theoretical probability is in favor of the player.

What the card counting proponents fail to comprehend is that progressive betting systems are not based on theoretical probability, but are based on empirical observation.

First, a definition of the word "empirical": Depending on experience or observation alone, without regard to science or theory. Many blackjack players, and many who write about the game, have observed that during actual play there are times when a player wins or loses many consecutive bets. They also have noted that these clusters of winning or losing bets occur with about the same frequency; a player is just as likely to experience a series of winning bets as he is a series of losing bets. Studies by mathematicians confirm this fact.

Based on these *empirical* observations, a player will win more by betting more while winning clusters are occurring, and will lose less by betting less (or not at all) while losing clusters are occurring.

Simply stated, proponents of progressive betting *never claim that they expect to win a bet after winning a previous bet* — the primary argument that card counting theorists used to reject the validity of this type of betting system. The card counters have never been able to accept the value of empirical observation, and continue to rely on theoretical and computer-generated simulations of actual play.

An interesting element of this continuing debate between proponents of either betting system is that attacks upon credibility have *always been one-sided*. Mr. Einstein, Mr. Dahl, and I have never questioned the value of card counting. It's always the card-counting theorists who spend time and effort to discount the claims of progressive betting proponents. Progressive system proponents, on the other hand, *never* question the theoretical basis of card counting systems, but offer their plan as an alternative to card counting because casinos have made counting a very difficult task due to changes in rules and "heat" from management, and because most players don't have the time, skill, or bankroll to be successful card counters.

Why are traditional card counters so defensive, and so quick to reject the thought that some other method of playing blackjack might be possible? Why can't they accept that empirical evidence might be practical and useful to the average blackjack player? As Yul Brenner, King of Siam in *The King and I*, once said, "'Tis a puzzlement!"

# Chapter Nineteen
# TABLE TACTICS

I hope that what you've read so far has convinced you that there is some merit in Positive Progressive betting, and that the recreational gambler has a better chance of winning if he uses the system that I recommend. But is this all there is to it? Will you be a consistent winner by simply following my betting system? I don't think so!

There are many more aspects to the game of blackjack that need to be considered, even by the occasional gambler, and especially by those who play on a regular basis.

Remember, the more often you play, the more often you are exposed to the casino's built-in edge over you. Perfect play will still allow the casino at least a one-half percent advantage over you. Perfect application of a good progressive betting system or a good card counting system may swing the advantage in your direction, but not for long, and not unless you play a flawless game and experience a bit of good luck along the way.

BUT, there are a few things that you can do to improve your chances of winning — things that aren't related to the rules of the game and aren't related to which betting system you choose to employ. I call them "table tactics," and devoted a chapter to them in *Blackjack for the Clueless*. I'll briefly review these tactics in the hope that they may give you the extra "edge" that makes you a consistent winner.

## 1. PLAY IN A COMFORTABLE ENVIRONMENT.

Every casino has its own personality. Some are noisy, hectic, and exciting. Some are sedate, dignified, and quiet. Some are friendly, and provide generous "comps" to loyal, red chip patrons. Some are oriented to "high rollers," and could care less if you're betting $25 a hand. There are as many different types of casinos as there are different types of people!

Your task is to find a casino environment that blends with your personality, that makes you feel comfortable, that allows you to concentrate on the game. Fish don't live in the desert, and elephants don't live in the ocean, so don't try to be a fish out of water or an elephant that swims the back stroke!

## 2. PICK THE BEST RULES.

Blackjack rules vary from casino to casino, and sometimes from table to table in the same casino. The best rules for players are as follows:

> 3 to 2 payoff for blackjack.
> Double down allowed on any two cards.
> Double down allowed after splitting a pair (including Aces).
> Multiple pair splitting allowed.
> Dealer stands on soft 17.
> Surrender allowed.
> Special promotions which pay bonuses for certain hands when no additional side bet is required. (Example: 2 to 1 payoff for a suited blackjack.)

Any variation in these rules will normally improve the casino's advantage over the player. Casinos that change the rules to improve their odds are usually located in areas where they have little or no competition. Luxury cruise ships on extended cruises are the most likely to be less generous with their game rules, as are casinos in isolated geographical areas that have no nearby competition. In general, your best bet is to play where many casinos are competing for the same customers.

3. PLAY AT A "HAPPY" TABLE. Losers usually aren't happy. Winners usually are happy, and it's not difficult to figure out if the players at a table are happy or unhappy. The signs are clear: Lots of chips in front of the players, conversation and laughter, players congratulating other players when they win — you get the picture. If you can, play at this type of table, rather than one where players are constantly reaching into their purses or wallets, complaining about the dealer's incredible luck, and criticizing other players for their Basic Strategy mistakes. If you think you can "turn the tide" by sitting down at a losing table, go ahead! It makes as much sense as leaning into a punch!

4. BE MENTALLY AND PHYSICALLY PREPARED TO PLAY. Blackjack is a tough game — anytime and anywhere. If you're not physically rested and mentally sharp, you're going to make mistakes that will cost you money. The casino doesn't care if you are tired, or sick, or mentally distressed, or drunk — just so you place your bets in a timely manner and don't cause a scene. You must be the judge and jury. If you can't play your best game, don't play at all!

5. DON'T FALL IN LOVE WITH A TABLE OR A DEALER. The cards don't know who's dealing them, and they don't know upon which table they are being dealt. I know this sounds silly, but

you would be surprised at how many players stay at a losing table because they like the dealer or because they *had* been winning at that table. If you're capable of entering a casino, you most likely have some method of transporting yourself from one table to another. Do so when necessary!

6. DON'T BE GREEDY. I honestly admit that my greatest fault as a blackjack player is my desire to win LOTS OF MONEY! I know that my playing skills are sound and that my betting system is profitable, and that over time I will win more than I lose by adhering to the plan that I recommend to others. I, like many others, sometimes *attempt* to win much more than I *expect* to win, and this occasionally turns a winning session into a losing session. These losing sessions usually occur because I raised my initial bet to a higher level before my bankroll was large enough to support the increase. Learn to enjoy the small profits, and you will be less likely to suffer the large losses.

In general, common sense will rule your actions in a casino — if you let your common sense express itself! Keep in mind that your two reasons for being in a casino — fun and possible profit — can be undermined by your inability to rationally control yourself. And there is only one person you can blame for your losses and your displeasure. Not the casino, not the dealer, not the other players, not your friend or loved one — just you!

# Chapter Twenty
# MONEY MANAGEMENT

Your primary motivation for playing black-jack should be *winning money*. Equally as important should be your ability to keep most or all of the money that you win.

I've had many players tell me that they "expect to lose," and consider it the price of playing in a casino. If you feel this way, don't even play in the first place. Let's face it: Without the betting aspect, blackjack is a pretty dull game. Why expect to pay money for the privilege of playing?

If you tell me that you don't care about the money and only play the game because it's fun and mentally challenging, then you've probably never played card games like bridge, rummy, canasta, or many others which really *are* fun and intellectually stimulating! Either play to win money, or don't play.

So, the principle reason you enter a casino is *money* — more specifically, winning theirs and not losing yours. Obviously the casino's reason for inviting you to the casino is just the opposite.

And casinos are *very good* at what they do! Based on their many advantages over you, they are much more likely to accomplish their goal than you are to accomplish yours. They design *every* game so that they have a built-in edge over you. They require that you convert your cash into tokens and colorful chips, in hopes that you'll forget that you're playing with real money. They provide an attractive environment staffed by handsome men and beautiful women who treat you as if you are one of their best friends. They entice you with promises of free food, lodging, and entertainment — as long as you keep playing. They offer you free alcoholic beverages in hopes of loosening your inhibitions, and your purse strings! They work very hard at accomplishing their only goal, which is *winning your money.*

Your task is to enjoy all of these pleasant amenities while at the same time not letting them accomplish their goal. A few simple rules will help keep you on the path to profitable play:

1. Never play with money that you can't afford to lose, or money that is allocated for other casino vacation expenses.

2. Be sure that your bankroll is large enough to support your betting preferences. If you're a "green chip" player, don't go to 'Vegas with a $500 bankroll and expect to play blackjack for several days. To be on the safe side — to insure that you have enough capital to play — your bankroll should be at least 40 times your minimum bet for each hour you plan to play blackjack. If you don't have enough cash, either lower your minimum bet or wait until you've saved enough money to sustain your level of play. The object here is to give yourself a chance to win, and you won't have this chance if your bankroll is too small to survive losing sessions.

3. Never enter the casino with more cash than you need to complete a session of play. The amount you need depends upon your level of play, your skill level, and the length of the session.

A famous gaming expert once suggested that the best bet in blackjack is to wager your entire bankroll on *one hand*. A skilled player using basic strategy only faces a .05% disadvantage on the outcome of one hand of play — almost a 50-50 chance of winning. You will either double your bankroll (or draw a blackjack and win even more) or go home broke.

Most of us don't want to play the game this way. We enjoy the casino environment, the hand-by-hand pursuit of our overall goal, and the thrill of the chase. But without an adequate bankroll there *is* no chase, so learn to apportion your money over the length of time that you plan to gamble.

3. Establish reasonable "win expectations." Don't expect to get rich every time you enter a casino. Since blackjack is a very volatile game, your win/loss record will fluctuate throughout a session. This book is devoted to teaching you how to maximize your chances of winning; you must learn to apply this information to the real-life game, and then establish goals which have a reasonable chance of being accomplished.

The amount that you hope to win or can comfortably afford to lose is a personal issue, based on your financial status, skill level, and conservative or aggressive manner. The important thing is to *decide in advance* where you plan to go with your game, and then stick with the plan. And remember, GREED has caused many winners to end up losers!

4. Never quit when you're winning! This sounds like a contradiction to previous advice, but it really isn't. Every experienced player will tell you that winning streaks occur. There are times when it seems that *you just can't lose!* Personally, I've won 20 hands in a row, won every hand in a six-deck

shoe, won consistently for hours, days, weeks at a time!

Granted, these streaks don't happen as often as we would like, but we must take advantage of them when they occur. Continue to play until the cards turn the other direction, and *then* quit. Don't expect your good fortune to immediately return, because losing streaks are just as likely to occur as winning streaks. Your job is to hold on to most of the profits that Lady Luck awarded you.

5. Don't abandon your plan because you're losing. Players often become discouraged when they lose hands that "the book" says they should win, and deviate from their game play in a desperate attempt to recoup losses. Increasing the bet or ignoring basic strategy — a condition commonly referred to as "Blackjack Fever" — will usually only worsen the situation. Either stick with your plan and accept that all players occasionally lose, or quit playing.

6. Don't play if you're not having fun! A basic premise of this book is that blackjack is a recreational activity. If you're not enjoying the game, simply quit playing.

However, if you're not really enjoying yourself, but you're continuing to win lots of money, then you might want to reconsider this last bit of advice!

Learn to apply these money management tactics, and you'll see a marked improvement in your gambling bankroll!

# Chapter Twenty One
# COMPENSATION PROGRAMS

It's possible to realize a profit even if you lose money while gambling in a casino. Sounds crazy, but it's true because casinos reward players for visiting their establishments.

Let's take a look at two different types of vacations: A golfer's vacation and a casino gambler's vacation.

You and a partner are avid golfers. You decide to spend three days playing golf at a major PGA course. Your expenses include hotel accommodations, meals and beverages, entertainment, greens fees, cart fees, equipment costs (gloves, balls, tees, locker room), not to mention the initial cost of clubs, bag, shoes, etc. It's likely that your daily cost of playing this game might exceed $500 per day.

Let's also assume that you had the best round of golf in your life! Or perhaps the worst round of golf in your life. In either case, your cost of pursuing your hobby *remains the same*. You still spend $500 per day, and the host — the owner of the establishment — congratulates you for your best round of play (or advises you to take lessons from the house pro — for a fee, of course) and sends you on your way.

Let's now look at the casino gambler's vacation. The initial cost of accommodations, food, and entertainment are similar. The cost of initial equipment and supplies is non-existent. You don't have to spend money to buy the "tools" that are required for other recreational activities.

We now assume that you had the best casino gaming experience of your life ! — or perhaps the worst experience you've ever had. In either case, it's likely that the establishment — the casino — will *reward* you for your efforts! It's likely that some or all of the expenses associated with your pursuit of your hobby will be paid for by your host.

How is this possible? The answer should be obvious. The casinos have a chance to win LOTS OF MONEY from you! Every casino has a built-in advantage on *every game* played, an "edge" that allows it the flexibility of giving benefits to players who frequent their establishment on a regular basis.

The golf course can only cover its cost of operation and draw its profits from the fees charged for the services rendered. They have no built-in advantage over the players, and neither profit nor gain from how well players play the game. They must make a profit from your use of their facilities, because they have no way of profiting from the game of golf.

SO . . . how do casinos decide how much they need to give back to their players to insure that they will continue to play in their establishments? The answer to this question is very complicated and confusing for lots of reasons, the main reason being that *they do what they have to do* to maintain a competitive share of the market in their gambling jurisdiction.

Casinos in highly competitive jurisdictions tend to be generous with their comps, while casinos that enjoy a monopoly tend to be very stingy with their free or discounted food, entertainment, or lodging.

In general, casinos will *give back* to their loyal customers about 20% to 40% of the amount that they *anticipate* winning from them. Their anticipated profit is the casino "edge" built into every game offered to their customers.

For example, in the game of blackjack most casinos figure to make about 1% of the total money wagered. In order to decide what comps should be rewarded to players, the casino figures out the *anticipated* profit by multiplying the number of hours played (about 80 hands per hour) times the average amount bet, times the anticipated profit from the game being played, times the percent of profit that they choose to return to the players in the form of comps. Understand? I told you it was complicated!

In regard to our two players on a casino holiday, we'll assume that they were progressive betting, were using the $20–$50 spread, and averaged $30 per bet. Each played six hours per day, averaging 80 hands per hour, and each was *expected* to lose 1% of the money wagered. We will also assume that the casino comps at a rate of 30% of the anticipated losses.

Consequently, the formula for calculating each player's compensation would be:

Eighteen hours (three days at six hours per day) × 80 (hands played per hour) × $30 (average bet) × 1% (anticipated casino profit) × 30% (comp rate) = amount of compensation awarded to player. This works out to be casino compensation of $129.60 to each player, for a total of $259.20.

Our players would receive this compensation

by being granted a lower rate on lodging, free meals, free entertainment, or a direct cash payment, depending on casino policy. If the casino were associated with a golf course, it's possible that our gamblers might receive free golfing privileges as well!

If you stop to think about it, casino gambling may be the *only* type of business that rewards participants for pursuing their recreational activities! Obviously our vacationing gamblers save money by taking advantage of comp programs. The downside is that they lose *as much or more* than the casino anticipates. But it's also possible that they will *win* money! In either case, the casino will still reward the players based on the comp formula. Comps are like "icing on the cake" for winners, and a "consolation prize" for losers.

In the initial paragraph of this chapter I said that it was possible to make a profit from gambling even though you lost while gambling. The profit that occurs is a result of the comps you receive, since in order to pursue your gambling hobby you would have to pay for food, lodging, and entertainment if comps weren't available.

I calculated the comps that would have been awarded to our three blackjack players in the 5,000 hands of play, and arrived at the following: The flat bettor earned $339.04 in comps, the progressive bettor earned $509.71 in comps, and the card counter earned $628.70 in comps. After subtracting losses from comps rewarded, we find that the flat better was still losing $270.16. The card counter had a net profit of $88.70, and the progressive bettor had a net profit of $479.71. Once again, the progressive bettor showed results that were superior to the card counter or the flat bettor.

To draw the most benefit from comp programs, always obtain a casino rating card before beginning play, always present it to the pit boss prior to placing a bet, and *never* continue playing just for the sake of being comped.

# Chapter Twenty Two
# APPLYING THE POSITIVE PROGRESSIVE SYSTEM

This chapter presents a step-by-step explanation of how to play blackjack with Positive Progressive betting.

1. ESTABLISH YOUR MINIMUM BET. The size of your minimum, initial bet should be determined by the size of your session bankroll. I recommend that your bankroll be at least 20 times (preferably 40 times) as much as your minimum bet for each hour that you plan to play.

For instance, if your minimum bet is $10 and you plan to play for four hours, your bankroll should be at least $800 ($10 X 20 X four hours).

2. PLAY WHEN THE CASINO ISN'T CROWDED. This is important for two reasons. First, our field tests show that the opportunity to benefit from winning clusters occurs more often when you play lots of hands per shoe. The more hands you are dealt, the more likely that strings of winning bets will come your way. Consequently, play at tables with six or eight-deck shoes, and play when no more than one or two other players are present.

The second reason to play during off-peak hours is because you need to be able to quit play and change tables if you lose four consecutive hands. It will cost you playing time and potential profit if the casino is busy and you have to wait for a seat at another table.

3. USE THIS BETTING PROCEDURE. The Positive Progressive system used in this book works as follows:

A. Decide upon and place an initial bet at the start of a new shoe (Example: $10.)

B. Once play begins, *increase* this initial bet by 50% if you show a net profit on a hand (Example: $10 to $15).

C. Continue to increase the bet *by the same amount* after each winning hand (Example: $10 to $15 to $20 to $25).

D. *Stop increasing* the bet after three increases, and let your maximum bet ride until you lose it (Example: $10 -$15 - $20 - $25 - $25 - etc.).

E. Any time you show a net loss on a hand, *revert back* to the initial minimum bet (Example: $10 win — $15 win — $20 lose — $10).

F. A "push," or tie with the dealer, is ignored for progression purposes, and the pushed bet should remain the same on the next hand.

G. Bet changes due to splits or double-downs are dependent upon the *net win/loss results* of the hand.

If you win a double-down, increase the bet to the next step. If you lose, decrease to the minimum initial bet. If you push, the bet remains the same as when the hand started. Don't forget to remove the additional bet you placed when you doubled on the hand, and start the next hand with the same bet that was up when the hand began.

If you win money as a result of splitting a hand, increase the bet by the prescribed amount on the next hand. If you lose money on a split hand, revert back to the initial minimum bet. If you push on a split hand (win one, lose one) the initial bet is carried over to the next hand.

Remember, the *net financial result* of a hand is always the key to bet increases or decreases.

7. BLACKJACKS. A *player* blackjack is treated like any other win, and a *dealer* blackjack is treated like any other loss.

8. BET INCREASES. *Never* increase the bet by larger increments than those described above, even if you win several bets on one hand due to winning splits or double-downs.

9. NEW SHOES. Always revert to the initial minimum bet at the start of a new shoe.

The preceding playing method can be applied to higher or lower initial bet amounts, just as long as the 50% increase and the three-step progression is observed. For example, if your bankroll is sufficient and table limits allow, you could employ a $20-$30-$40-$50, a $50-$75-$100-$125, or a $100-$150-$200-$250 progression.

If you're a "red chip" player ($5) I recommend a $5-$7-$9-$11 progression, since casinos usually don't allow 50-cent bets due to the difficulty of paying off player blackjacks.

If you find yourself at a $25 minimum table, I recommend a $25 - $35 - $45 - $55 progression.

Due to the less than 50% increase for winning bets caused by chip denominations for $5 and $25 initial bets, I recommend that these progressions not be employed unless absolutely necessary.

Keeping in mind that the initial bet is based on initial bankroll, you may wish to *alter* the initial bet while a session is in progress. Let's assume that your initial bankroll was $800, your initial bet was $10, and that you've completed playing three hours of a four-hour session. You count your chips, and find that you are $800 ahead — your bankroll has doubled!

So what do you do? Some of your options are:

1. Continue to play in the same manner until the end of the session.

2. Immediately quit play, and enjoy your profits.

3. Reduce your initial bet by 50%, thus improving your chances of retaining most of your profits (or winning a bit more) through the end of the four-hour session.

4. Double your initial bet because your bankroll has doubled, and continue at this level until the end of the session or until you lose the profits earned from the start of the session.

I consider *any* of the above options to be acceptable. After all, different strokes for different folks! My personal inclination is to follow Option #4 and double my initial bet, since I'm a very aggressive player. But I must honestly admit that I often regret making this decision!

Now let's look at another session — same bankroll, initial bet, and time played. Only this time you find yourself *losing* $400 — half your bankroll. Your options are:

1. Continue play in the same manner, and hope that you hit a series of winning clusters.

2. Quit play, accept a $400 loss, and live to fight another day.

3. Reduce your initial bet by 50% since your bankroll has been reduced by 50%.

4. Double your initial bet, and hope for the best.

I consider any of the first three options to be

acceptable (I usually follow Option #1), but would be VERY CRITICAL of your decision to select Option #4. If you learn nothing else from reading this book, learn that you should *never exceed* the betting limits dictated by the size of your bankroll. It's the same as "leaning into a punch" and almost always leads to you being knocked out of the game.

There's another playing tactic that deserves mention if you're having a profitable session: Play *two* hands.

This tactic adds a bit more excitement to the game, and allows you to put twice as much money in action without twice the risk, since winning and losing hands often offset each other.

Our studies show that two progressive players playing against the same dealer often experience very different win/loss results, so it's very possible that one hand can be drawing clusters of winning bets while another hand is losing minimum bets. Or that both hands could be enjoying winning clusters because the dealer is busting more often than normal.

Since I'm often faced with the problem of playing in crowded casinos (It's the only game in town!) I often use the two-hand tactic. If I lose four consecutive hands on one of the hands I'm playing, I quit play on that hand and continue playing the other hand. I'm not forced to move and find another open table.

When playing two hands it's important *not* to intermingle profits and losses. Play two separate spots, and keep a separate chip stack for each. If one hand continues to lose, quit playing it until the start of a new shoe.

A final suggestion for experienced card

counters: If you're a proficient counter, there's no reason why you can't use Positive Progressive betting and apply your card counting skills *simultaneously*. Simply use the progressive system as your betting spread while the count is neutral or negative. On those rare occasions when the count skyrockets, an unusual increase in the wager will usually be ignored by the dealer or the pit boss since you have established a pattern of increasing your bet in spite of the count.

This method of disguising your skill level should be more effective than other methods currently employed, such as increasing your minimum bet at the start of a shoe, intentionally misplaying a hand when the pit boss is watching, or pretending that you made a mistake when you change Basic Strategy on the basis of the count.

If you are a "green chip" ($25) card counter, use a $20 to $50 Positive Progressive system, and that occasional increase to $75 or $100 will be seen as an "inspirational" increase rather than a counter's increase. Try this system for a while, and you'll find that the minimum bets that you *anticipated* losing might be as profitable as the card counting system that you expected would make money for you!

So that's it — my method of Positive Progressive betting. I realize that much of the preceding information seems a bit unscientific, and I've conducted no long-range studies to verify that these money management and playing techniques are fool-proof. But I've used these techniques for many years and they work for me. I hope they work for you!

# Chapter Twenty Three
# SUMMARY OF RESULTS

The overall intent of this book is to illustrate that flat betting and progressive betting *do not* achieve the same outcome, and that the use of a specific progressive betting system will consistently produce financial results that are superior to flat betting.

A brief summary of the studies conducted shows that these conjectures have merit:

1. Initial study (2,300 bets).

Both the flat bettor and the progressive bettor lost money, but the progressive bettor *lost less.* Card counting was not part of this study.

2. Fred Renzey's manually-dealt sample (792 hands).

Again, both players lost, but the progressive bettor *lost $507 less* than the card counter. The flat bettor was excluded from this study due to changes in Basic Strategy employed by the card counter.

3. 5,000 consecutive hands of play (5,554 bets).

The progressive bettor showed a net loss of $30, which was *$580 less than the flat bettor's and $510 less than the card counter's losses.* End-of-shoe results show that the progressive bettor was ahead of the casino more often than the other two players, and required a smaller bankroll than the other two players.

4. Progressive Quit Points.

The 5,000-hand study strongly indicates that

*all* players would have improved their win results had they used this table tactic. Also, when quit points were honored by all three players, the Positive Progressive bettor *won more* than the flat bettor or the card counter. This study also illustrates that running totals are improved dramatically and total bankroll required is decreased dramatically when quit points are employed.

5. Field tests (approximately 700 bets).

In the first field test (250 hands), the progressive bettors lost *$250 less* than the flat bettors.

In the second field test, 345 bets were placed. The three progressive bettors collectively *won $465 — $115 more than the flat bettors.*

In the third field test, the progressive bettors *won over $300*, but the recording of the results of consecutive play was disallowed by casino personnel.

6. Fred Renzey's 1,004 hand trial (approximately 1,100 bets).

Fred changed the amounts bet by the card counter and the flat bettor in an effort to "equalize" the total amount wagered by each player. In spite of these changes in format, the Positive Progressive bettor lost *$675 less* than the flat bettor, and *$2,535 less* than the card counter.

7. Bootlegger's 1,011 hands of play.

This practicing card-counter played 21 shoes of manually-dealt blackjack, using the KO system. Although the "run" was negative for all players, the Positive Progressive bettor lost *$700 less* than the $30-per-bet Flat bettor, and *$20 less* than the KO system card-counter

8. Advanced card counting system (1,101 bets).

Due to a suggestion by another casino gaming expert, I up-graded the counting system used in the 5,000-hand study, and played an additional 20 shoes (991 hands) of blackjack. The Positive Progressive bettor won $830 — *$400 more than the flat bettor, and $1,330 more than the card counter.*

9. Computer game simulation (962 bets).

I programmed the computer to play the player's hands, and played 20 shoes of blackjack. The Positive Progressive bettor *won $90*, the $20 Flat bettor *lost $80*, and the $30 Flat bettor *lost $120.*

10. Comparison of progressive betting systems.

Comparing the win-loss results from the first 20 shoes of the 5,000-hand sample — negative for all players — the Positive Progressive bettor lost *$315 less* than the Dahl System player, and *$285 less* than the New York System player.

11. Computer simulated long-run play.

An analysis of 200,000 computer generated hands of play produced results consistent with all preceding short-run studies.

The studies in this book analyzed the results of over 13,600 blackjack bets, plus computer "sims" of 350,000 hands of play. In *every* case the Positive Progressive bettor showed more positive financial results than the flat bettor or the card counter. Need I say more?

Yes, I *do* need to say more! Much more research should be conducted to verify my findings and conclusions. I hope that this book will encourage others to investigate progressive betting and its potential benefits to the average blackjack player.

This book is only the "tip of the iceberg," an iceberg than may someday sink many ships piloted by traditional blackjack theorists. Time will tell . . .

# SUGGESTED READING

The following list of books, magazines, and newsletters provide, in my opinion, the most accurate and up-to-date information about the game of blackjack. Although I disagree with some of the opinions offered by some of the authors, I enjoy reading their work and respect their knowledge of the game of blackjack.

## BOOKS

Bourie, Steve. 1999 *American Casino Guide*. Dania, FL: Casino Vacations, 1998.

Dahl, Donald. *Progression Blackjack*. Secaucus, NJ: Citadel Press, 1995.

Canfield, Richard A. *Blackjack Your Way To Riches*. Secaucus, NJ: Lyle Stuart, 1995.

Grochowski, John. *The Casino Answer Book*. Chicago, IL: Bonus Books, 1998.

Grochowski, John. *Gaming*. Elmhurst, IL: Running Count Press, 1996.

Grochowski, John. *Winning Tips for Casino Games*. Lincolnwood, IL: Publications International Ltd.

Humble, Lance & Cooper, Carl. *The World's Greatest Blackjack Book*. New York: Doubleday, 1980.

Perry, Stuart. *Las Vegas Blackjack Diary*. Pittsburgh, PA: ConJelCo, 1997.

Reber, Arthur S. *The New Gambler's Bible*. New York: Crown Trade Paperbacks, 1996.

Renzey, Fred. *Blackjack Bluebook*. Elk Grove, IL: Chicago Spectrum Press, 1996.

Scoblete, Frank. *Best Blackjack*. Chicago: Bonus Books, 1996.

Scoblete, Frank. *Guerrilla Gambling*. Chicago: Bonus Books, 1993.

Tamburin, Henry. *Henry Tamburin on Casino Gambling*. Greensboro, NC: Research Services Unltd., 1998.

Tamburin, Henry. *How To Win: Reference Guide to Casino Gambling*. Greensboro, NC: Research Services Unltd., 1996.

Thomason, Walter. Ed. *The Experts' Guide To Casino Games*. Secaucus, NJ: Carol Publishing Group, 1997.

Thomason, Walter. *Blackjack for the Clueless*. Secaucus, NJ: Carol Publishing Group, 1998.

Wong, Stanford & Spector, Susan. *The Complete Idiot's Guide to Gambling Like a Pro*. New York: Alpha Books, 1996.

Wong, Stanford. *Professional Blackjack*. La Jolla, CA: Pi Yee Press, 1994.

# MAGAZINES

*Casino Player*. Casino Journal Publishing Group. (1-800-969-0711).

*Midwest Gaming & Travel*. Midwest Gaming. (1-507-835-1662).

*Chance & Circumstance*. Paone Press. (1-800-944-0406.)

# NEWSLETTERS

*Blackjack Forum.* RGE Publishing. (1-510-465-6452).

A word of caution: There are hundreds of books and thousands of articles written about blackjack. Many are republished without update or revision, and many contain outdated or obsolete information. And many contain *incorrect* information! Select your resources carefully, and verify what you read!

There are also many people who choose to take advantage of the ignorance and gullability of people who wish to improve their casino gambling experience. Be skeptical of those who promise you big wins and want to charge you lots of money for their "secret formula" for success. Everything you need to know about the games is available from your local library or bookstore, and doesn't cost much.

# GLOSSARY OF BLACKJACK TERMINOLOGY

ACTION: The amount wagered over a period of time.

ANCHOR: The last player to the dealer's right at a blackjack table.

BACK COUNTING: A card counting technique wherein the player does not enter the game until the count is in his favor.

BANK: Whoever covers all bets (usually the casino).

BANKROLL: The total amount that the player has to spend on a session of play.

BARRING: Permanently ejecting a player, often for counting cards.

BASIC STRATEGY: A blackjack playing system that provides the long run, optimal way to play, based on the player's cards and the dealer's exposed card.

BET: The player's wager.

BETTING SPREAD: The ratio between a player's minimum and maximum bet.

BLACKJACK: The most common name for the game of 21.

BLACKS: Casino chips valued at $100 each.

BREAK/BUST: When the dealer's or player's blackjack hand exceeds 21 points.

BURN CARD(S): The first card(s) discarded from a deck or shoe.

BUY-IN: The amount of cash exchanged for chips at the initiation of play.

CAGE: The cashier's section of a casino.

CARD COUNTING: Keeping track of the cards that have been played.

CASINO HOST: A casino employee that caters to big bettors.

CASINO MANAGER: The chief casino executive on duty.

CASINO RATE: A reduced hotel room rate offered to good customers.

CHECK: Another name for a chip.

CHIP: The monetary token used in lieu of cash.

COMP: Complimentary lodging, food, services, or gifts provided by the casino to qualified players.

COUNTER: A player who applies a card counting system.

CUT: To divide the deck into two parts after the shuffle.

CUT CARD: A solid colored card, usually plastic, used to cut the deck.

DEAD CARD: A card already played or discarded.

DEALER: The person who deals the game.

DOUBLE-DOWN: A blackjack rule which allows the player to double his original bet and be dealt one, and only one, card to his hand.

DRAW: To receive cards from the dealer after the original deal.

DROP BOX: A repository for cash, markers, and chip receipts on a gaming table.

EDGE: To have an advantage in a game.

EVEN MONEY: A bet that pays you back the same amount that you wagered, plus your original wager.

FACE CARDS: The jack, queen, or king of any suit of cards.

FIRST BASE: The first blackjack player on the dealer's left.

FIVE-COUNT SYSTEM: A blackjack play strategy based on counting 5s.

FLASH: To see the dealer's unexposed card.

FLAT BET: Betting the same amount on every hand.

FLOORMAN: A casino executive who supervises part of a pit and is under the supervision of a pit boss.

FRONT MONEY: Cash required and deposited with the casino in order to receive comps.

GREENS: Chips valued at $25.

GRIFTER: A gambler who cheats.

GRINDER: A small money bettor.

HARD HAND: A blackjack hand without an ace, or a hand where the ace can only be counted as one point.

HEAD-UP: Playing alone against a dealer.

HIGH ROLLER: A gambler who plays for high stakes.

HIT: A single card received by a player or dealer.

HOLE CARD(S): The unexposed card(s) in a hand.

HOT: A player or dealer on a winning streak.

HOUSE: The gambling establishment; the casino.

HOUSE EDGE: Mathematical advantage the casino has over the player.

INSURANCE: Betting that the dealer has a ten-card under his ace.

JUNKET: A short gambling trip, often paid for by the casino.

LAYOUT: The design or diagram imposed on a casino table game.

MARKER: A casino document that allows a player

to draw chips against his credit or cash on deposit.

MARTINGALE SYSTEM: A progressive betting system that instructs the player to double the wager after each loss.

MATCH PLAY CHIPS OR COUPONS: A comp given to a player which allows him to match the amount of the chip with a like amount of cash on a single wager. If the player wins, he is paid the combined amount of the match play chip and the cash wager.

MECHANIC: A person (usually a dealer) who is proficient at cheating.

NATURAL: Same as a blackjack; a two card total of 21 dealt on the first round of play.

ODDS: The probability of winning a given bet.

PAINT: Any picture card.

PAIR: Two cards of the same rank.

PAT HAND: A hand to which no further cards need be drawn.

PEEKING: A form of cheating whereby a dealer peeks at the top card to determine whether or not to deal a second.

PERKS: Minor comps received by a player.

PIT BOSS: A supervisor of one or more gaming tables.

POINT COUNT: The total number of points in a player's hand. Also, a blackjack card counter's summation.

POSITIVE PROGRESSION: A progressive system wherein the player increases the bet after a win, and decreases to the minimum bet after a loss.

PUSH: A tie between the dealer and the player.

PRESS: To increase a wager after winning a hand (usually double the original wager).

REDS: Chips valued at $5 each.

RICH DECK (SHOE): A partial deck or shoe that has a disproportionately high percentage of face cards and aces.

RUNNING COUNT: The count maintained in blackjack card counting systems as each card in dealt.

SESSION: The amount of time devoted to play without leaving the casino.

SHILL: A casino employee who poses as a player in order to attract other players into a game.

SHOE: The container from which multiple-deck games are dealt.

SHUFFLE: The mixing of cards before the deal.

SOFT HAND: A blackjack hand with an ace which is counted as 11 points.

SPLIT: Splitting a pair to create two separate hands.

SPREAD: In blackjack, the difference between a card-counter's minimum and maximum bet.

STAND: The decision to receive no further cards.

STIFF: A blackjack hand with a hard point count of 12 to 16 points.

STRATEGY: A method of play based on long-term probabilities.

SURRENDER: A blackjack rule that allows you to give up half of your original bet for the privilege of not finishing the hand.

TACTIC: A short-term system or strategy.

THIRD BASE: Same as anchor (blackjack).

TOKE: A tip, or a wager placed for the dealer.

TRUE ODDS: The ratio of the number of times one event will occur to the number of times another will occur.

UNIT: The dollar amount of a basic bet; one chip.

WALK AWAY A WINNER: The objective of *every type* of casino gambling!

# ADDITIONAL RESOURCES

Current and up to the minute information about casinos and casino gambling is available from the magazines, periodicals, newsletters, distributors, and publishers listed below. Write or telephone them, and they will be happy to send their catalogs or subscription requirements.

*Atlantic City Insider.* 8025 Black Horse Pike, Suite 470, West Atlantic City, NJ 08232. Monthly newsletter. 800-969-0711.

*Blackjack Confidential Magazine.* Eight Issues Annually. P.O. Box 8087, Cherry Hill, NJ 08002-0087.

*Blackjack Forum.* RGE Publishing, 414 Santa Clara Avenue, Oakland, CA 94610. Quarterly guide for serious players. 1-510-465-6452.

*Casino Journal's National Gaming Summary.* Weekly summary of gaming news. Fax 1-702-253-6805.

*Casino Player Magazine.* 8025 Black Horse Pike, Suite 470, W. Atlantic City, NJ 08232. Monthly casino gaming news, books, and software. 1-800-969-0711, Fax 609-645-1661.

Casino Vacations. P.O. Box 703, Dania, FL 33004. Steve Bourie's American Casino Guide, plus Selected books and software. 1-800-741-1596, 954-989-2766, Fax 954-966-7028.

Gamblers General Store. Large selection of books, videos, software, and equipment. 800 South Main St., Las Vegas, NV 89101. 1-800-322-2447, 1-702-382-9903.

Gambler's Book Club. 630 S. 11th Street, Las

Vegas, NV 89101. Large selection of books, videos, and software. 1-800-522-1777.

Gambler's Edge. Books, videos, and software. 4344 S. Archer Ave., Chicago, IL 60632.

*Goodtimes Newspaper.* Gaming news. 1-901-755-6622, Fax 1-901-753-9816.

*Gulf Coast Casino News.* Gaming news. 141 C De-Buys Road, Gulfport, MS 39507.

*Las Vegas Advisor.* Huntington Press. 3687 S. Procyon Ave., Las Vegas, NV 89103. Monthly newsletter & book sales. 1-800-244-2224.

*Las Vegas Insider.* P. O. Box 29274, Las Vegas, NV 89126. Monthly newsletter & book sales. 1-520-636-1649.

*Las Vegas Sports News.* Newspaper. 1-800-32-LUCKY.

*Lottery & Casino News.* Newspaper. 1-609-778-8900.

Research Services Unlimited. Books & Videos by Henry Tamburin. P.O. Box 19727, Greensboro, NC 27419. 910-8568708, Fax 910-856-2311.

Paone Press. Newsletter and book sales by Frank Scoblete. Box 610, Lynbrook, NY 516-596-0406, Fax 516-596-0646.

Pi Yee Press. Newsletter and book sales. 7910 Ivanhoe #34, La Jolla, CA 92037-4502. Fax 1-619-456-8076.

Your comments regarding the content of this book would be most appreciated. I'll respond as time allows.

Walter Thomason
PO Box 550068
Ft. Lauderdale, FL 33355